Footnotes on the Sands of Time

FOOTNOTES ON THE SANDS OF TIME

Occasional Essays
from
Before and After Retirement

J. Russell Elkinton, MD
MACP, FRCP

Emeritus Professor of Medicine,
University of Pennsylvania
Editor Emeritus, Annals of Internal Medicine,
American College of Physicians

The Cottage Press
Lincoln Center, Massachusetts

For information contact:
The Cottage Press
P.O. Box 6135
Lincoln Center, MA 01773
(617) 259-8771

ISBN 1-882063-30-9
First Printing
Printed in the United States of America

Books by the Author

*The Body Fluids: Basic Physiology
and Practical Therapeutics*
    —with T. S. Danowski, MD
        (1955)

*Who Shall Live?: Man's Control
Over Birth and Death*
        —with working party of the
        American Friends Service
        Committee
        (1970)

The Quaker Heritage in Medicine
        —with Robert A. Clark, MD
        (1978)

*Bird On A Rocking Chair: A Miscellany
of Occasional Essays From Family
and Professional Life*
        (1988)

CONTENTS

PART II (1987 - 1994)

Acknowledgements

Many of these essays have been published previously and I am grateful to the editors and copyright-holders for permission to reproduce them, in whole or in part, in this volume.

The following essays appeared in the ANNALS OF INTERNAL MEDICINE of which I was Editor at the time: *Genetics and Ironing, or the Two Cultures and the Physician; Editor Garland and* The New England Journal of Medicine; *Beards, Flowers, Drugs, and Love; The Case of the Itching Tattoo; Things That Go Bump in the Night.*

The LINCOLN REVIEW published *Everglade Interlude: Awaiting the Wail of the Limpkin in a Cypress Swamp; The Nightingales: Lincoln Library's Lovely Lively Literary Ladies; Avalanche of Paper, Deluge of Words; Watching a Pair of Lesser White-crested Birdwatchers; From Crete to Arizona - Gathering Time; Bird in a Wheel Chair: The Decelerating Years in a Home Away from Home.*

The essays that appeared first in the CARLETON-WILLARD VILLAGER were: *Daughter in College, or a Tale of Two Cities and Luggage ; The Rise and Decline of the Age of Antibiotics; Books and the World Inside One's Head.*

The cartoons and line-drawings not drawn by the author but taken from his collection of cartoons clipped over the years without record of their source, the artists, where their names are legible, are acknowledged in the preceding copyright acknowledgements.

The critical comments of my wife, my children, and my friends, have been extremely helpful and I wish to thank them. Finally, to Mary Ann Hales of The Cottage Press I am most grateful for her great efforts in editing and publishing this volume.

J. R. E.

Any reasonably long life, looked back upon, irresistably suggests a journey. I see these stories, inventions on a base of experience, as rest stops, pauses as I tried to understand something or digest some action or clarify some response.

—Wallace Stegner, in the Foreword to
Collected Stories (1991)

Preface

The cordial reception given to my first collection of essays, *Bird On A Rocking Chair: A Miscellany of Occasional Essays from Family and Professional Life*, has encouraged me to produce a second volume of similar material. Here it is.

This set of essays is divided into two parts. In the first, are occasional essays written during the last decade of my professional life as an academic physician and medical editor, and when our children were growing up. The subjects, in the main, are glimpses into the life of our Anglo-American family with overtones of my editorial activities. In the second part, the pieces have been written more recently during what I have labelled "the decelerating years"—the later and less active years of retirement. In consequence, the subject material in this part is retrospective, looking back and ruminating on some of the experiences and interests that have come my way in a rich and satisfying life.

Drawings and pictures can enliven the written word and again I hope that they do so here, The majority of the drawings are from my own amateurish pen but I have leant on a few professionals for help from theirs. A good cartoonist holds the mirror up to life to show the foibles, the ironies, the paradoxes, that characterize the human condition; laughter helps us to accept what we see.

Once more, to Teresa, my dear wife and companion for more than half a century, to our children, and to our grandchildren, Miranda, Rebecca, Rosalie, Barry, and Reed, who are learning who they are and what to do with their lives, and finally to my friends who are sharing the satisfactions and burdens of our "decelerating years", I dedicate this book.

J. Russell Elkinton

Bedford, MA
May, 1994

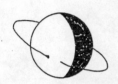

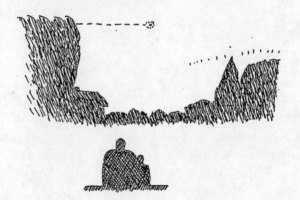

Part I

(1959-1970)

1

Something New Under the Sun

It was clear and cold in the early dawn of that day, October 16th, 1957. Joe and I in our bathrobes sat huddled under a blanket on the back steps with our faces to the sky. Behind the trees across the garden the eastern horizon was just beginning to glow with that clear pale white light that, on an absolutely cloudless night, heralds from afar the approach once more of the life-giving sun. Overhead the stars in their constellations twinkled and glittered in the purple-black of the still-reigning night. Against this scene, daily re-enacted over an eon of time, we are keeping a rendezvous with something new (literally) under the as-yet-unrisen sun. That something is the first earth-orbiting satellite made and launched by man.

"The newspaper predicts, Joe, that the rocket will appear at 5:01 high in the northeast towards the zenith, about 60 degrees up, moving southward. Watch the sky in front of those high tulip trees below the garden, look for a moving light". We waited, and shivered, and wondered if we would see it and if we did, what it really would look like. The minute hand reached 5:00, crept on slowly to 5:01, and beyond—second af-

ter second. And suddenly—there it was, on time, keeping its
rendezvous! Emerging from behind the lofty tree-tops, a
bright white light, a small glowing ball like Venus, the evening star, moving steadily across the vault of the high eastern
sky. Eerily it progressed on its undeviating course, a new and
audacious interloper against the background of the familiar
stars. Through Orion it passed, outshining Betelgeuse, on towards the southeastern sky. And then, ere the second minute
had passed, it was gone—vanished into the shadow of its
mother planet, the Earth.

Called *Sputnik* by the Russians who launched it eleven
days before, it was the first of many rockets hurled into space
during the two years since that day, by the Soviets in Siberia
and by the Americans at Cape Canaveral—*Sputniks, Explorers,
Vanguards, Luniks, Pioneers, Discoverers*—probing fingers of
man's restless mind! Some of these have gone higher, some
have sent back more information, some have escaped Earth's
gravity entirely and gone on to orbit about the sun, some have
hit or circled the moon. But this was the first and we had seen
it! Like the first wheel turning on a prefashioned axle, like the
first alphabet conveying thought, like the first steam-engine
moving under its own power, like the first airplane flying for
the first time at Kitty Hawk, like the first atomic nuclear explosion lighting up the Nevada sky, this too was something
under the sun really new!

"An experience to remember, Joe!"

Moylan, Pa.
November, 1959

Postscript, 1994: Since that first man-made orbiting satellite crossed the sky, now almost four decades ago, the space
age has erupted with almost unbelievable scientific and tech-

nical sophistication. Men have walked on the Moon, unmanned probes have landed on Mars and made close-up visits—Mariners and Voyagers—to the rest of the planets of the Solar System. Venus has been mapped by radar, the moons of Jupiter and the rings of Saturn have been photographed in close detail. Astronomical observations of the cosmos have been freed from the limitations of the Earth's atmosphere by orbiting detectors of infra-red rays, gamma rays, x-rays, Big Bang residual microwaves, and visible light from the far reaches of the universe collected by the orbiting Hubble telescope.

Perhaps of more immediate importance to mankind is the effect of orbiting satellites on our own planet Earth. Telecommunication satellites in fixed orbits provide instant contacts between all parts of the globe. Survey satellites permit constant surveillance of military and ecological phenomena—weather, ocean currents, and conditions on land.

But the most important effect of the new space age on humankind is the provision of a new perspective. For the first time man sees *in toto* the planet Earth, that unique vivid blue and white jewel of a globe suspended alone in the black void. It is our only home—we had better take care of it.

All this has come from "something new under the sun."

Earthrise on the Moon

Trafalgar Square —
as Picasso might see it

2

London, Picasso, and the Horse's Mouth

Two girls in bright green raincoats under pastel-shaded umbrellas crouch against the great stone lion at the foot of Nelson's column. The rain slants down from the grey cloud to mingle with the water of the fountains, white showers thrown upward from turquoise basins. In the background the tall red buses with ceaseless motion circumnavigate the periphery of the square, and motionless the tall white spire of St. Martin's-in-the-Fields keeps watch over the blocks of stone that long have displaced the fields of waving grain. Down Whitehall the sun breaks through the clouds sending shafts of light up the street, rain drops sparkle as they splash and bounce on the gleaming pavement, and the highlights glisten on the wet black backs of the sleeping lions of Trafalgar Square. The rain fades away; the girls with the bright umbrellas move on and merge with the river of humanity that flows without end in this timeless city of London.

Back in London again! After three years absence we eagerly absorb with every sense the sights and sounds, the

smells and feelings, of this wonderful city. Down the river
from the spires of Westminister we go by boat, under bridges
old and new, past St. Paul's and the Tower, past Dickensian
inns and wharves, past Elizabethan river-steps, past new sky-
scrapers clothed in scaffolding and impudently pushing their
way upwards over the ancient scene, past modern docks,
cranes, warehouses, ships, to Greenwich, meeting place of
East and West, longitude zero,—all on the River Thames, har-
bor to the world! And up the river past Chelsea Embankment,
Battersea Park, Strand-on-the-Green, Kew, and Richmond, to
Hampton Court with its gardens for kings and its maze for
small boys (Joey promptly got lost). Through the greenery of
West End parks, St. James's, Hyde, Regent's, past the newly
renovated John Nash crescents and terraces, through the City
on the Strand, past Liverpool Street Station to the grey stone
wilderness of East London (vain prophesy: "'when I grow
rich,' say the bells of Shoreditch"). And back again to the Hay-
market, the theaters, and the bright "Bovrillian" lights of Pic-
cadilly, bullseye of nocturnal London.

But have we sensed the real London, seen the city as it
really is? Vain question for each seer perceives a different city,
a city unique unto himself. Down at the Tate Gallery hang the
paintings of an artist who paints not what he sees but what he
thinks; the painted object takes only the form that he perceives in his own mind—Picasso. But what a painter and what
a mind! Surely no one else has ever perceived and thought of
a woman in a red arm-chair, a woman weeping, or even a
kitchen, as Pablo Picasso has perceived and thought and
painted them. So the city must be perceived differently by
each perceiver, although probably seldom with the perceptual
abandon of a Picasso!

Alec Guiness playing the artist in the motion picture of
Joyce Cary's story, *The Horse's Mouth*, brings much the same
message: each individual perceives and experiences reality in

his own way and to this he must be true. We saw this movie, appropriately enough, in the little theater high up in Hampstead amidst the artists and near their annual sidewalk exhibition. Hampstead is a lovely vantage point for any individual viewer of London. Here the summer sun lights the many old doorways with their newly painted doors of yellow, black, lavender, or pink (what would Samuel Johnson have said to Boswell as he jogged along Flask Walk in his sedan chair?). Up from the Heath come the noise and music of the Bank Holiday carnivals and fairs, of Ferris wheels and merry-go-rounds, of Londoners disporting themselves between the hills of Highgate and Hampstead. And beyond, out over the Heath, the great city is spread before us. Londonium grown up, not old—and still growing!

We return to warmth and welcome in the family home in Hampstead. Old friends and old sights have given the city back to us again, the city perceived differently by each of us but by virtue of our humanity, common to us all.

London
August, 1960

8

D.N.A.

THE BEGINNING OF LIFE

as seen by

Pablo Picasso   Watson and Crick

3

"Genetics and Ironing"

The Two Cultures and the Physician

During a recent vacation from college our daughter announced that she had to spend the evening "doing genetics and ironing." Now here is a phrase that epitomizes the situation of us all—modern men caught up in the accelerating whirl of the scientific revolution, modern physicians faced with the challenge of understanding molecular disease. Our daughter studies genetics in order to comprehend the new world in which she lives; she does her ironing to prepare for practical social living. Modern man is buffeted by a veritable hurricane of new scientific knowledge of the macrocosm and microcosm and struggles to trim the boat with the esthetic, social, moral, and spiritual insights of the humanities. The modern physician finds himself in the midst of a revolution in the life sciences that daily advances his understanding of the mechanism and treatments of disease, and daily forces him to reorient accordingly his care of patients.

The "two culture" schism in our society between science and the humanities has been set forth forcefully by Sir Charles Snow in his now-famous Rede Lecture of 1959. There is, Sir Charles believes, a serious lack of communication and understanding between the scientist and the non-scientist. In a world rapidly being transformed by the scientific revolution such a division holds great hazard for our Western civilization. Many thoughtful observers have recognized this dangerous dichotomy and many a flag of truce and reconciliation is being raised amidst the snowballs flying from each side of the "Snow-gap."

A similar effort is needed in the world of medicine. For medicine has its own "two culture" schism. There is a rising note of concern among medical leaders and educators over the rift between the medical scientist and the medical practitioner, between the investigator and the healer, between the science and the art of medicine. These two facets of our profession, the art and the science, have been with us for a long time but the rift between them has been accentuated of late by a variety of factors: the great sums of public money being poured into medical research, the public pressure for progress in the treatment of specific diseases, the prestige value of the image of the researcher, and, most of all, the astounding revolution in the biological sciences that has taken place in the last fifteen years.

The world in which the physician finds himself has become increasingly complex, be he practitioner or investigator. It is a world in which poliomyelitis is not only a disease (happily now rare) in a sick patient but a virus that is described in terms of crystallography, physical chemistry, electron microscopy, immunology, virology, and genetics. It is a world in which radio telemetry figures in communication not only with satellites orbiting the globe but with diagnostic radio capsules orbiting the duodenal loop. It is a world in which electronic computers are applied not only to the guidance of rockets and telephone bills to their respective targets but to the assistance of physicians to their patients' correct diagnosis. Yet the busy practitioner's days are filled with the ever-present and real needs of Mr. Doe's nagging epigastric pain, Mrs. Doe's perennial backache, and Junior's sore throat. And Mr. and Mrs. Doe and Junior are more than systems of molecules, cells, and organs, more than helices of native or subversive viral DNA, more than cells with mitochondrial engines, more than organs of unbelievable complexity; they are human beings with problems emotional, mental, and spiritual, as well as physical. Here the doctor is meeting the two cultures face to face, and needs to draw as deeply as possible on both his scientific knowledge and his human empathy and understanding.

The medical world, as well as the world at large, urgently needs to bridge the cultural gap. The physician-scientist must remind himself of the enormous difficulties that face the physician-practitioner in translating scientific knowledge into useful treatment of the diseased human being. The physician-practitioner must make allowance for the tremendous and accelerating complexities that face the physician-scientist. In varying proportions every physician must be both scientist and healer. For yesterday's research is today's treatment, today's research will be tomorrow's treatment; in the physician, the scientist and the healer are one.`

March, 1952

Postscript, 1994: Since the above essay was written more than three decades ago, the issues facing the physician and medicine have changed. The two cultures now are overshadowed by a third "culture." It is the "culture" of socioeconomics, of money, management, competition, cost-control, universal coverage, and how it all is to be paid for. Whatever comes out of President Clinton's current drive for health care reform, and of the tortuous manipulation thereof by the Congress, there remains paramount the physician's need to know more about disease and the patient's need to be treated as a whole person. Care of the patient is the primary target—and the patient is the public.

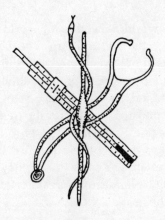

PHYSICIAN: SCIENTIST *AND* HEALER

Is the clinician a biochemist, a biophysicist, a biologist, a pathologist, a psychologist, a psychiatrist, a social scientist, a statistician? In my view he is none of these and at the same time he must be something of all of them. . . . As a scientist and a scholar, he must be aware constantly of the limits of his knowledge, of human error in observation and recording, of the constant need to look critically at what one believes one knows, and to be alert to the clues which may lead to new knowledge. At the same time in his role as a participant-observer, not as a spectator of the human comedy, he must act as best he can with the methods, instruments, and ideas of the moment, and he must act now and not tomorrow. He cannot postpone, he cannot wait for certainty, or at times, for even reasonable confidence. He must do what he can to relieve the pain, distress, and suffering of his patient with the information, knowledge, skill, and wisdom that he has acquired. —John Romano, *Journal of the American Medical Association*, 1961.

4

Iona to Coventry

A Fresh Wind Blows from the Western Isles

The lonely track winds through the peat and heather, past the deserted crofts on the ancient hills, and on to the lighthouse by the sea where the dark rocks jut into the western ocean. This is the tip of the Ardnamurchan peninsula, the western-most point of the mainland of Scotland. To the north the ragged peaks of Rhum and Eigg, and of the Cuillins on Skye, are painted by the sunset in diminishing intensities of purple and blue—a veritable Maxfield Parrish painting of the storied Western Isles. The sun itself is setting in a blaze of light behind the golden cloud bank that lies above the unseen Outer Hebrides just over the horizon. Past the low-lying forms of Col and Tiree, the long rock cliffs of Mull run to the southwest toward the Dutchman's Hat, a tiny distant island-rock marking the turn of the coast toward Staffa and Iona.

Iona is out of sight but not out of mind. From a voyage around Mull some years ago with an old friend, an Englishman long familiar with Scotland and the Western Isles, I remember a small stone church glistening in the rain on the green sward behind the shore, a shore that we could not reach because of the heavy seas. It was a church small but not insignificant for Iona is the site of the first Christian church and community in Scotland. Founded in 563 A.D. by St. Columba from Ireland, Iona shared with the earlier Christian Celtic communities of St. Dubricius in Wales and the Roman Christianity shortly to be brought to Saxon England by St. Augustine in 597, the establishment of the Christian faith throughout Britain. Thus, the little church at Iona was one forerunner of the churches great and small, the cathedrals and parish churches, the chapels, the quiet meeting houses—all the places of Christian worship within these British Isles. In this year of our Lord, nineteen hundred sixty-two, the mighty new cathedral of Coventry opens its doors in evidence that the creative spirit of modern man is still at His beck and call.

In the saddle of Beinnna Seilg, the double-peaked mountain behind our village of Kilchoan, little Ghleann Locha, cupped between the lonely banks of rock and heather, reflects back the blue sky of the Western Isles. Here son Joe and I climb to fish for the loch's piscine denizens who leap and snap at everything except our lures and flies. We and the fish are in a lonely land, empty save for history. To the north lies the Isle of Skye of the Clan Macleod, and to the east, Loch Moidart and Loch Sheil where Bonnie Prince Charlie landed for the ill-fated attempt of 'the forty five." To the south is the Isle of Mull of the Clan McLean and Tobermory on the Sound of Mull beneath whose waves is the final resting place of the treasure galleon of the Spanish Armada—a grim reminder of Philip of Spain's futile attempt, ten centuries after the founding of Iona, to impose his own brand of Catholicism on the Prostestant England of Good Queen Bess. And on our little loch a pair of red-throated divers serenely float, oblivious, as are the fish beneath them, of either the histories of men past or the desires of men present.

The waves and rocks, the winds and skies, the birds and fish, must be much the same as on the day when St. Columba came to Iona. But the minds of men are not the same because of the new thought that flew in on the wings of the wind from the Western Isles.

July, 1962

5

Black Mountain: Then and Now

Steadily the T-bar of the ski tow draws up the slopes of snow—Tessa and I, Gwyn and Joe. Steadily the prospect broadens and the valley falls away as we ascend the southern end of Black Mountain. To the east across the higher valley stands Doublehead Mountain, clad in spruce and snow; to the southwest beyond the lower valley Passaconway and ridge after ridge of the White Mountains run in ever-bluer ripples to the distant horizon. At the top of the tow, around the shoulder of the mountain, we get a glimpse of the monarch of them all—Mount Washington, a great white Moby Dick looming against the cold blue of the northwest winter sky. Then amidst the throng of the many-colored skiers we turn from the distant view and start our run down the mountain. With a schuss, a turn, a run with the wind in the face, and a halt for breath, we experience the old exhilaration that comes with the skis that give wings to the feet in the mountains in wintertime.

Tessa learned the love of skis in Switzerland, I here in the White Mountains. Twenty-eight years ago my roommate in medical school, Andy Burgess, first brought me to his family's farm at the foot of Black Mountain. For three winters and springs Andy and I spent all the time we could spare, skiing in these mountains: Doublehead, Wildcat, Tuckerman's Ravine and Headwall, and even the summit of Washington. But our favorite was Black Mountain. With lunch in pack, with new Norwegian skis and bindings, we would don creepers and take the long trail upward to the northeast ridge of Black Mountain. There, over the top, was a faery upland of semi-open snow slopes of green spruce and white birch, of view incomparable: to the northwest, Washington, Wildcat, and the Presidential Range, to the east the State of Maine spread out before us as far as eye could see. There, utterly alone in a white and pristine world, we would swoop and turn and climb again for hour after joyous hour. At the end of the day, through sunlight and April snow showers, we would run the long trail home, refreshed beyond measure.

Black Mountain is less lonely now. And the sport of skiing is conducted in a different manner—all downhill dash, no uphill work. And other things have changed. Beside my daughter's modern boots and safety bindings, my old Norwegian ski equipment is quite passé. Sinews are older and muscles are stiffer. He and she who once were the gay young skiers, running the slopes with verve, looking forward to life with zest, run slower now, and with caution. The tight control is gone, the abandon abandoned. But flying past us, making three runs to our one, are our children. It is they who ski with verve; it is they who ski down the mountain with controlled abandon; it is they who face life with the zest of youth. We are content.

And so the day ends. We take our leave of Black Mountain, our muscles aching, our youth relived, our spirits renewed.

Jackson, N.H.
March, 1963

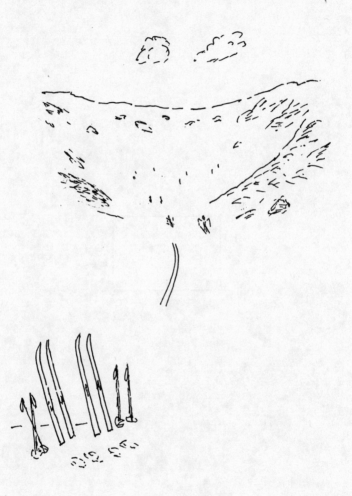

JFK

6

Days of Hope, Days of Grief

> No man is an iland, intire of itselfe... any
> man's death diminishes me because I am in-
> volved in mankinde; and therefore never
> send to know for whom the bell tolls; it tolls
> for thee.
>
> —John Donne

The whispered word came, two long days ago as we
waited in the airport: "the President has been shot in Texas."
And before the flight commenced we knew that President
John Fitzgerald Kennedy was dead. Flying into the Southland
beside a dull red sun sinking into a gloomy bank of cloud and
haze, the very sky held a portent of blood and a foreboding of
bigotry and strife. The stunned mind refused to accept the in-
credible fact that he was gone, and not until the return flight
yesterday could the fact begin to be grasped. Coming in over
Washington in a driving storm of rain, wind, and lowering
cloud, one began to grapple with the question, why, why,
why? Why was his body already lying here in the city where

he had fought his battles as he led the nation? Anguished over this question, we left the dim grey dome of the Capitol outlined against the black sky of the oncoming storm, and flew on home in a turbulence of storm without that matched well that of the storm within.

This morning in Meeting, as in every church in the land, we the people examine our souls in anguish and offer up our prayers for redemption and unity. And even as we watch on the television screen the long slow sad procession from the White House to the Capitol, comes the fantastic word from Dallas of the assassination of the alleged assassin. With tension and grief we see the mortal remains of John F. Kennedy, to the roll of muffled drums, move along the same Pennsylvania Avenue that three short years ago he so eagerly rode to his Inauguration.

On that bright sunny winter day of January 20, 1961, when the white snow covered the city and and the wind blew cold and clean, John Kennedy took the oath of office to become the 35th President of the United States. We watched the scene then on the same screen that we view again today. In a world taut with the tensions of the cold war, threatened with the thermonuclear doom of a hot war, bound with the shackles of seemingly inexorable hatreds, that day was a day of hope. Here was a man with courage, with intelligence, with the vigor of youth, with the compassion of experience. Hear him as he spoke:

> Let the word go forth from this time and place, to friend and foe alike, that the torch has passed to a new generation of Americans...

> So let us begin anew...Let us never negotiate out of fear, but let us never fear to negotiate...

> Now the trumpet summons us again...not as a call to battle, but to bear the burden, "rejoicing in hope, patient in

tribulation," in a struggle against the common enemies of man: tyranny, poverty, disease, and war itself.

The magic of television brought to us all the little things of that bright day: the exchange of friendly talk between the old President and the new as they sat waiting, the proud and happy smile of Jacqueline Kennedy, the young and beautiful new First Lady, the alarming column of smoke (due to a short circuit) arising from the lectern during the overly-long invocation, and the touching episode of Poet Robert Frost trying to read his special poem for the Inaugural and hampered by wind and brilliant sunlight. We saw, too, that evening the entry of the handsome young President and his beautiful wife onto the balcony overlooking the Inaugural ballroom, and the whole world seemed again to be a place of youth and gaiety and, above all, hope.

There were little happenings today, too: 3-year old John, Jr., clutching his mother's hand as they stood before his father's coffin and bending back his head to look up into the great dome of the Rotunda, Caroline smoothing her white gloves and looking to her mother for her cues as together they knelt to kiss the flag-draped coffin, Jacqueline Kennedy's gracious turning beside her limousine to speak a few last words to the new First Lady and President Johnson. These little things make poignant the stark tragedy of these terrible days.

Tomorrow, John Fitzgerald Kennedy, in the presence of prime ministers and princes, of kings and common men, will be laid to rest. It will be a day of mourning by the nation and by the world that he served so well. He who brought a new exercise of reason into the irrationalities of international relations, he who achieved a restraint on the mad rush to nuclear armament, he who withstood successfully all pressures for impetuous action from left and right in the crisis over missiles in Cuba, he who knew that civil rights of all men must be championed and did so—will pass into history. He who brought the bright light of hope and integrity to the affairs of men goes down in a black cloud of evil deeds and foul suspicion rising from the heart of Texas to cast a shadow across the land. A sad day for America, a day of grief.

The eulogies in the Rotunda today included these words:

> He gave us of a good heart from which laughter came. He gave us of profound wit from which a great leadership came. He gave us of a kindness and strength fused into a human courage to seek peace without fear... And now that he is relieved of the almost superhuman burdens we imposed on him, may he rest in peace.

For each of us the bell has tolled.

Moylan, Pa.
November 24, 1963

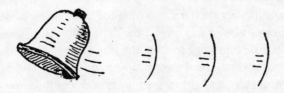

Postscript, November 22, 1993: Now, thirty years to the day after that terrible event, we ask why, to so many of us, its vivid memory and strong emotions remain? What was it about John Fitzgerald Kennedy that moved us so strongly, then and now? During the intervening years theories of assassination conspiracy have proliferated (still unproven) and iconoclasts have been at work. We know that his personal life was flawed, that his political accomplishments were not all successful, that he might, or might not, have become a great President. But he was young, handsome, intelligent, and he had charm—an incandescent charm—that was felt by all Americans. This charming young President lifted our spirits and, in the dark time of the Cold War, gave us hope. Then came the bullets that gave us days of tremendous grief—grief for his family, grief for our country, grief for everyone.

Now, in a time, not of Cold War, but of economic, ethnic, and nationalistic conflict on a global scale, we have a new young President who again gives us hope. May he fare better than did his young predecessor of thirty years ago.

7

Everglade Interlude

Awaiting the Wail of the Limpkin in a Cypress Swamp

Straight as an arrow runs the dirt road south into the heart of the Everglades. It is a dusty line bisecting a two-dimensional world of waving grass and sky. In the distance to left and right lie many a hammock capped with palms and many a head of grey-green cypress festooned with hanging moss. And ever in the ditch by the side of the road flow the dark waters of the swamp, waters that teem with forms of aquatic life hidden from human eyes in the brown waters below.

The human eyes are few. We are two non-native couples traveling down that road: Jerseyman Jack—born a naturalist and raised a lover of the Everglades—and his English Tessa, my English Tessa and Pennsylvanian I. Jack and his Tessa are out to show us their beloved tropical Florida, we are out to see new birds, and Jack is out to record on tape certain sounds of nature including the childlike cry that the limpkin makes at dusk, Hence our detour down this side-road, hence our lingering till the setting of the sun. Other humans are fewer. Two college boys from Oklahoma in a dilapidated and failing Cadillac are catching snakes; one sits on a front fender with burlap bag and forked stick and leaps on unsuspecting reptiles slithering off the side of the road. We view their catch with cautious interest and push their stalled car into life. One bronzed native Indian in a pick-up truck stops to inquire if we had seen his hound—"lost him on a coon hunt last night down this a'way." No hound at hand.

We come to a pool in the cypress swamp, dark and mysterious. The fish are jumping. In the hidden depths behind the moss and vines a host of birds are wading and roosting. Over the tree tops in the light of the setting sun, the night herons, white ibises, and wood storks are flapping to their grounds. By the edge of the pool a green heron squawks and warily keeps his distance. Jack sets his microphone, for surely here will the limpkin cry. The first sound—recorded in perfection—is the long haloo of the coon hunter for his wayward hound. Try again. The call of a crested flycatcher, the "klop" of the rising fish, the sudden rattle of night herons in their herony—but no limpkin cries.

The rustle of wings over the tree tops dies away; silence and darkness settle over the swamp-land. The wail of the limpkin, like the hoped-for soaring circle of the swallow-tailed kite and the bright flash of the painted bunting must wait for another visit and another year. We turn to the homeward way, happy in our human fellowship and content with our reception by the world of swamp and sky.

March, 1964

Postscript, 1994: Thirty years later we can see in what has happened to Florida and the Everglades a paradigm of what is happening to much of our planet: too many people, too great a need for water and food, too much pollution, too much development, too much encroachment on the natural environment.

On the day in 1964 described above, our friends had taken us across the Everglades to Marco Island on the Gulf coast. Marco's beach of white sand fringed with palm trees and Australian pines was pristine, wild, and utterly deserted—not a building or human habitation to be seen. Today Marco Island with its houses, hotels, and marinas has been called "the Miami Beach of the West." Now the Everglades themselves are threatened with drying up as the water from Lake Okeechobee and the underground limestone aquafers that flows on through the Everglades to Florida Bay, is extensively diverted to the large sugar plantations north of the Everglades and to the burgeoning populations of the cities of South Florida.

Belatedly efforts are being made to save the Everglades, but the flora and fauna have suffered. No longer in the evening do such large flocks of ibises, woodstorks, and herons fly in to roost in the tree tops of the cypress swamps. And no longer, perhaps, does the limpkin wail—or fail to wail—as it did (or didn't) those thirty years ago.

8

Daughter in College

A Tale of Two Cities and Luggage

The speaker at the parents' dinner on Wellesley's Commencement Weekend gave the theme. But from Father's point of view, just one word epitomizes those four years that Daughter spends in college—luggage. From the first trip with the tyro freshman, through the comings and goings of each vacation and year's end, to the seasoned senior's final homeward trek—luggage! Suitcases, bicycle, hockey stick, record player, book bag, guitar, skis, ski boots, skates, binoculars, typewriter, pictures, lamps, more suitcases, more books (loose), more dresses (unpacked), and so on—seemingly without end. All these are to be carried, stowed, and transported in various combinations in automobiles, airplanes, trains, or buses, between Philadelphia and Boston, between Boston and Philadelphia. Daughter to be met, daughter to be seen off—always welcomed on arrival, always missed when gone, and always with luggage.

For Father there are a number of other landmarks of Daughter's college career beside the supervision, nay the handling, of luggage and the regular semi-annual communications from the College business office. There is, for instance, Sophomore Fathers' Day. For this occasion, in the spring of the second year, an entire April weekend is given over to feting Dad on campus with a series of bright events. The dance on Saturday night with Dad as escort brings back to him his own college days with a whiff of nostalgia for the girls, the bands, the dances, the bright fresh look of the world, in those far-off salad days. Can this lovely girl in my arms really be my daughter? The shock of this reflection adds caution to Father's performance of the twist, danced (in place of the Charleston) with determination but not with abandon—too easy to visualize the vertebrae parting company. But part they did not, and the evening was a great success.

Then there are a few family weekends, during Spring Vacations, spent skiing together in the mountains of New Hampshire and Vermont. But for most of the four years Mother and Dad touch Daughter's life at college only from a distance by letter and during occasional flashes of personal contact during vacations. For the rest we hear of the full life that really constitutes her college career: of history and literature, of language and philosophy, of reading in the "Libe" and late nights on papers, of concerts and plays, of travels back and forth along the Route 16 Harvard-Wellesley axis, of the duties and responsibilities of being House President. Then suddenly Commencement Weekend arrives.

The lovely young ladies in the black gowns are our daughters "going down"—as the Baccalaureate Sermon puts it—"like Moses, Jesus, and Zarathustra, into the world" (feminine titters, 380 girls strong). McGeorge Bundy gives a short, keen, witty Commencement address that is a poignant reminder of the great and able young leader whom he served and who came to the Presidency and left it so tragically, all within the compass of our daughter's four short college years. And so she receives her diploma—an outward sign that she who left us as a girl returns as a woman, eager, joyous, having learned so much, having so much yet to learn, and primed, we hope, to be a student of life for a lifetime.

The garden parties and banquets are over, the farewells are said, and there remains as in the beginning—luggage. In a veritable deluge of rain, every item mentioned in the first paragraph is damply stowed in the car, and Father retires for the last time to the men's washroom in the dormitory to remove and replace every stitch of his soaked clothing. And then— with the luggage—we are off. Our daughter's college days are over.

June, 1964

Postscript, 1994: Four years ago Daughter's daughter (our granddaughter) followed her mother's example and "commenced" from Wellesley, this time with the aid of First Ladies Barbara Bush and Raisa Gorbachov. Mrs. Bush concluded her address with the comment that, if the spouse of a future President should ever ask her for advice about housekeeping in the White House, she would be glad to give all the help possible to *him*—shreiks of female delight from the entire graduating Class! And then as before, time for Granddaughter's luggage to be fetched away—but this time, not by Grandfather.

9

A Clear Day in Shropshire

Westward on the high-hilled plains
Where for me the world began,
Still, I think, in newer veins
Frets the changeless blood of man.
—A. E. Housman: *A Shropshire Lad*

Last night on the boards at Stratford we heard King
Henry IV thunder at Prince Hal and Falstaff and meet re-
bellion in his realm from across the Wye and Severn. Today in
Shropshire, across the Severn, we scanned the mountains and
valleys of Wales whence came the doughty Owen Glendower
to challenge, five centuries before, the King of England.

Between the busy cities of the Midlands and the Welsh
border lies Shropshire, a lovely land of long valleys, tiny
fields and hedgerows, and high ridges covered with bracken
and heather. Beyond the Long Mynd, the moorland roof-tree
of the shire, rises another ridge, the Stiperstones. Here along
the crest, amidst the heather, stands a series of rock out-
croppings of dark limestone and white quartz in weird and

jagged silhouette against the sky. The highest of these, the Devil's Chair, is a spot surrounded by mists of legend and superstition, as set forth in the novels of Mary Webb. Here also is the site of one of the most superb and far-flung views in England.

Today, on one of the clearest days that we can remember in this storm-swept land, our friends, John and Lou, and Tessa and I crossed the Severn at Bridgenorth (King Henry's rendezvous) and journeyed through the lanes of Shropshire to the Stiperstones to climb to the Devil's Chair. Behind us, over the ridge of the Long Mynd, were the tips of the Midland landmarks whence we had come: the Wrekin to the northeast, the Clent Hills, the Brown Clee, the Malverns. Before us, in a wide arc from south to west to north, lay the mountains of Wales in ever-receding ridges of lighter and lighter blues—here dark under the shadow of the clouds, there bright with patches of sunlight, and all swept with the fresh wind from the unseen western sea. Fifty miles to the south the sharp point of Skirrid-fawr stands as a sentinel at the entrance to the Black Mountains whose long line of purple ends in the abrupt drop of Hay Bluff and Lord Hereford's Knob. Then come the distant Brecon Beacons, the nearer high black silhouettes of Radnor Forest and Clun Forest, distant Plynlimon, and the jagged twin peaks of Cader Idris, capped with clouds. Beyond the Arans are the twin tips of the Moelwyns, and past the nearer ridge of the Berwyns the faint glimpse of a blue line under clouds suggests the mighty Snowdon—a full sixty miles to the northwest. Beyond the Berwyns the line of the North Wales mountains runs down to the River Dee. Across the wide flat plains of Cheshire and Staffordshire are dimly seen the refineries of Merseyside and the towers of Liverpool—fifty miles and more away.

Here, under one sweep of the eye, lie a hundred miles of England and Wales. Here lies the real stage of history that fed the pen of Shakespeare. Here lies a beloved land where still "frets the changeless blood of man." Here lies a heavenly view from the Devil's Chair.

Belbroughton, Worcestershire
August, 1964

THE DEVIL'S CHAIR

Low on the opposite ridge, the larch woods still kept their breathless May freshness, reaching up wistfully toward the gaunt, unchanging heights and the Devil's Chair. Among them the fir-trees reared their tarnished blue-green—sullen, archaic sentinels of death in a world of immaculate, indomitable youth. A soft, strong wind blew from the west, quick with the year's promise, brimful of meadow and mountain scent. Large clouds continually came up from beyond the Chair, darkened it, swept over the valley, and suddenly disappeared like conjured ghosts as the warm air struck them.

Deborah sat down beneath the signpost... She looked across at the Devil's Chair—dark and shining as a night-sapphire. It seemed to her that there was no hostility now between the two ranges, between the towering throne and the small white cross. Always before, she had superstitiously regarded the Chair as wholly evil, the Flockmaster's signpost as wholly good. Now she saw good and evil mingled. Instinct told her that the two visions were one. She was content with the balance of life as she found it, being dimly aware that the terror and the beauty intermingled in something that was more wonderful than beauty.

"The thorn blows late," she murmured, with the patience of one that has come through tumult and found peace.
—Mary Webb, *The Golden Arrow*

Joseph Garland, MD

—Courtesy of J. E. Garland

10

Editor Garland of the *New England Journal of Medicine**

This month, for the first time in 20 years, the masthead of *The New England Journal of Medicine* appears without the name of Joseph Garland as Editor. In its place is that of Franz J. Ingelfinger who brings to his new post a wide experience as physician, teacher, an editor for *The Year Book of Medicine*, and former member of the Editorial Board of the journal he now directs. To Dr. Ingelfinger we extend all good wishes for a successful voyage over the editorial seas.

The retirement of Dr. Garland marks the end of one of the most successful editorships in the history of medical journalism. During his tenure the *NEJM* has become a national and international, rather than a regional, journal, and its circulation has soared close to the 100,000 mark. The reasons for this success are clear: excellence of content of the *Journal* and timeliness in meeting the needs of the profession. These qualities are to be found in the great variety of original articles, reviews, case reports, editorials, letters, and other features that come down each week from the heights of the Hub to the Journal's subscribers. The *NEJM* has indeed achieved the goal that its editor set for it, "to offer in each issue something of value to each reader who is really interested in keeping up with the times not only in his own area of interest but in others."

But the signs of a great editor go beyond the formal content of his journal; his personality comes forth clearly but unobtrusively on the printed page. We shall miss Dr. Garland's perceptive and pithy Yankee wit—hung as garlands on many an editorial and editor's note. Above all we shall miss his "wordsmanship;" as he himself expressed it:

> Finally there are the pleasures—the true editorial joys—that come with the exercise of wordsmanship. Wordsmanship does not only apply to dictionary definitions but to the general employment of these parts of speech and their suitability for the function that they are intended to perform—making them into phrases and sentences; their compression into abbreviations, their fusion into cryptic groups of initials and their expansion even to the point of utter verbal fission.

Examples of Dr. Garland's wordsmanship are legion and are cherished by all collectors of editorial Garlandiana. Such items range from famous editorials to whimsical medical reporting. There was, for instance, the editorial elaborating on "Wordsmanship, No Less" in which Dr. Garland explored the uses and abuses of the suffix "ship" as pertaining to the use of "relation" versus "relationship." He concluded his editorial thus:

> The case in favor of relation and against relationship except in a restricted sense having thus been clearly presented and incontrovertibly proved, it may be pertinent to recall a luncheon-

table conversation about the sinking of the Titanic that took place in the Harvard Club of Boston, on the anniversary of that melancholy event. "I had relations on the Titanic," one discussant modestly admitted. "With whom?" was the spontaneous interrogation of his fellow Harvardmen, striving for their own scholarly version of oneupmanship.

Then there was his editorial "The Wearing of the Genes" addressed to the relation of mutation rate to temperature of the testes; he closed with:

> The medieval European codpiece, or anterior trouser flap, is cited as a possible safety valve or ventilating apparatus, and it is well known that among the kilted Scots a man's a man for a' that. Under the circumstances it is a little bewildering for modern man to reconcile the necessity of keeping his jeans up and his shirt on with that of also keeping his genes cool, located as they are in the prescribed anatomical areas.

Many, many other editorials on a multitude of subjects have revealed Dr. Garland's bent for the succinct, the pithy, the humorous, that has shown him for what he is: the Yankee master of the written word. Presented as they were in the customary cloak of anonymity, some of these editorials may not have come from the pen of Dr. Garland. We may have arrived at erroneous conclusions, despite the clear kinship of these unsigned turns of wit with those more formal pieces to which he has put his name. In that case, we can at the very least praise him as an astute collector of wit shaped in fine prose.

Over the years Joseph Garland has maintained a cordial friendship with his great counterpart on the other side of the Atlantic, Sir Theodore Fox, long Editor of *The Lancet*. This relation(ship) was celebrated in the columns of the *NEJM* by Dr. Garland's famous account of the British-American Chipmunk Discovery Expedition in which he details the search from

Massachusetts to North Carolina by Editor Fox for a glimpse of that "indigenous rodent;" Editor Garland threatened a return Loch Ness Monster-Flyfishing Expedition (which unfortunately was never launched). More recently he greeted *The Lancet's* invasion of North America with his editorial entitled "Operation Beachhead" in which he welcomed *The Lancet* and hinted at a counterplan for a London edition of the *NEJM*.

No account of Dr. Garland's success as a medical editor would be complete without reference to his sure touch with, and fondness for, puns and light verse—usually to be found in the correspondence columns and often pinning some fluttering correspondent to the board. But such light touches, as well as his deft use of the felicitous phrase on the editorial page, has always been balanced by the multitude of serious and important medical articles Dr. Garland has set out as the real meat and drink in this great medical journal; surely in this lies the greatness, and much of the joy, of Joseph Garland's editing. As he retires from the *NEJM* editorial scene, may we wish him many years of the happy editorial horsechestnutmanship about which he has regaled us so delightfully:

> I remember well one such addict to horse-chestnutmanship (horsechestnuts carried in the pocket to ward off rheumatism) who averred that he had thus carried a buckeye, or a succession of them, continuously for six years, during which time he had been absolutely free from rheumatism.
>
> "And had you been greatly troubled before that," I asked.
>
> "That's the most remarkable thing of all," he replied. "It's retroactive."
>
> And perhaps the same may be said of the editor's joys and rewards.

Thank you, Dr. Garland, for sharing with all of us so fully your joys as editor; may your rewards be commensurate.

Philadelphia, Pa.
July, 1967

[Footnote: *This essay, first published as an editorial in the *Annals of Internal Medicine*, was written with the Associate Editor, Dr. Edward J. Huth, as co-author.]

"Troublemaker!"

11

Beards, Flowers, Drugs, and Love

In diversity among men lies the evolutionary strength of the race, and who differ more from the mainstream of human life than the "Flower People," the denizens of Hippieland? What are these young people with the flowing hair, the bizarre costumes, the aversion to soap, the special lingo, and the disdain for the ways of their elders, trying to tell us? And what do those of us who are middle-aged and "square" members of an older generation have to say to them?

To those who are parents of teen-agers attracted by this "new world of freedom," these are not academic questions. Nor are they for the rest of society, including the medical profession. What is so wrong with contemporary life that causes this particular group of young people to throw overboard most of the accepted standards and aims of their elders and to seek solace in drugs, sex, and freedom from any sort of responsibility? The answer, of course, is that plenty is wrong and the hippies are not the only ones who are worried. Ours is a world in which religious beliefs are less secure, moral standards have deteriorated, bigotry has become ever more apparent, the gulf between the affluent and the poverty-stricken has widened, and violence and a dehumanizing war have reached new and frustrating intensities that seem to baffle utterly both men of peace and men of war. Is it any wonder that thinking members of both generations, young and old, hippies and nonhippies, become depressed—at least in moments of fatigue, of low blood-sugar, and in the small hours of the night? Yet life goes on; man keeps on trying.

In their own way the hippies are trying too. They are asking us to reexamine the conventions, the rigidities, the hypocrisies of a materialistic way of life that has contributed to the "bind" in which we find ourselves. Their queries and their proposed alternatives have not lacked publicity—perhaps because of the flamboyant nature of their way of life; analyses of the hippie "subculture" have flooded the newspapers and magazines of the land. Serious as are the hippies' indictments of society's evils, it is their proposed alternatives that cause the most concern to us as parents and as physicians. The older generation, admittedly bearing a heavy responsibility for the plight of the world today, does not see that the answers lie in the euphoria of marijuana, psychedelic "trips" with LSD or amphetamines, in a "love" that is equated with completely depersonalized and promiscuous sexual experiences, or in total abdication from doing the work of the world. These alternatives to the "square" life offer no real solutions to society's ills and only can hold deep tragedy for those who adopt them and for their families.

The use of marijuana and of psychedelic drugs appears to be increasing among young people of high school and college age. The argument rages as to whether or not smoking marijuana (cannabis) leads to the use of stronger and more dangerous psychedelic drugs and to narcotic addiction. In view of the doubt on this issue, the legal penalties for even the possession of marijuana seem unduly harsh. In any case, the psychological dependence and the artificial escapism that come from the use of marijuana are hazardous, and these hazards are in no way mitigated or excused by comparing them to a socially accepted ethanolic counterpart. The use of lysergic acid diethylamide (LSD) has been promulgated as "mind-expanding" and as leading to profound artistic and spiritual insights. But there is evidence that LSD carries greater danger in the form of immediate or delayed psychoses and of chromosomal damage with the possibility of long-term genetic effects. Such dangers seem a large price to pay for artistic or spiritual insights that apparently have produced as yet no recognizable masterpieces. As for the amphetamines, particularly Methedrine or "speed," their use intravenously appears to lead to the total disintegration of the so-called "speed freak" with a rapidity that has alarmed even the hippies themselves.

These specific organic and psychological hazards are by no means the only dangers to the health of the hippies. The squalor and unhygienic environment into which they take themselves carry their own toll of infection and malnutrition. Add to these the hepatitis and venereal diseases that are the side effects of a life of drugs and sex, and the total price in broken health to these young lives becomes very heavy indeed.

Yet perhaps the greatest tragedy lies in the social sphere: the alienation of children from parents, the teen-agers who run away from permissive homes that seem loveless and empty of meaning, the brutal end that has come to a few, the anguish of bewildered parents fearing for their children lost and wandering in an alien, urban, and hostile world. These are the extreme results of youthful decisions to resign from the world as it is—to "cop out." Russell Baker has written with humor of the impass that would obtain if everyone "copped out." But this is no laughing matter to the young people who choose this road, or to their parents. Such parents, faced with a virulent new form of the perennial revolt of youth and wracked with worry and usually with guilt, cling to the hope that somehow experience—that hard teacher—will bring home the lesson before it is too late, that work is more satisfying than indolence. The example of personal standards, plus an understanding affection that constantly keeps open the lines of communication between parents and children, is perhaps the best preventive measure—short of changing the world. Changing the world, of course, is what is needed most.

"Love" is one of the words heard most frequently on the tongues of the Flower Children. As they use the word they appear to mean not only attraction between the sexes but tolerance for people of differing views. But the love that is needed so sorely in the world today is more than mere tolerance, more than just the absence of hate; it is understanding and compassion and a desire to serve outside oneself. This is the kind of love that will lead to the growth of purpose and sanity in the lives of all men everywhere, east and west, black and white, young and old—and with beards and without.

December, 1967

Postscript, 1994: Has the world changed for the better, now that a quarter of a century has passed? And what has become of the Flower Children? The answer to the first question is—yes and no. As for the second, the long-haired young people in revolt in the 1960s have become short-haired middle-aged responsible citizens of today, worrying in turn about *their* children. Inevitably the hippies matured—to the relief, and perhaps to the enlightenment, of us oldsters, as well as of themselves.

GENERATION GAP OBSERVED

Profile of two generations separated by a gap, or maybe only a yawn:

Fears: The older generation's chief fears are hair and Communism. The younger generation lives in dread of college-admission offices and the draft...

Ambitions: The chief ambition of the older generation is to become young. The chief ambition of the younger generation is to stay young long enough to make man perfect...

Vices: The older generation likes martinis. The younger generation likes noise.

Joys of life: The universal joys among the older generation are two—driving and consuming.... The younger generation also finds pleasure in taking trips, motorcycles, beaches and clothing of orthodox unorthodoxy.

Government: The older generation's pet hate in Government is the Internal Revenue Service; the younger generation's is the Pentagon. The older generation is resigned to Government; the younger generation, fortunately, can never be resigned to anything....—Russell Baker, Observer: profile of a gap. *New York Times*, October 24, 1968.

12

The Case of the Itching Tattoo

The tattooed lady, that legendary attraction of the circus, had better stay out of the sun—she might get the itch. For years it has been known that tattoos containing red pigment may develop an itching eczema, warty nodules, and even sarcoid-like granulomas. Because the red pigment employed in the main by tattoo artists is cinnabar—mercuric sulfide—this allergic reaction usually has been assumed to be a manifestation of mercurial hypersensitivity set off by a subsequent exposure to mercury in any of a variety of forms. But such exposure has often been hard to establish, and concomitant systemic sarcoidosis has never been proved; thus the cause of the reaction in such cases has remained somewhat a mystery.

In a paper published in the *Annals of Internal Medicine* Goldstein has solved the case of the itching tattoo. And he has done so with a deftness that would do honor to the Master Sleuth of Baker Street and that would (as usual) bring amazement to the admiring Dr. Watson and consternation to Inspector Lestrade. Presented with fifteen tattooed patients who had itching and nodular reactions in the red areas of their tattoos, Dr. Golstein ran the culprit down: it was cadmium sulfide. None of his patients had received mercury in any form; their tattoos had all been exposed to sunlight just before the localized reaction began. Following the clue that yellow tattoos were known to be light sensitive and the yellow pigment used was cadmium sulfide, he showed [1] that commercial "red" tattoo pigment actually had some yellow cadmium sulfide mixed in with the red mercuric sulfide to make the color brighter, [2] that tattooed skin biopsied from three of his patients contained traces of cadmium sulfide, and [3] that experimental tattoos on the skin of mice made with commercial "red" pigment reacted to sunlight while those done with chemically pure mercuric sulfide did not.

Furthermore, cadmium sulfide is the photosensitive substance used in photoelectric cells. As Sherlock Holmes would have said: "Elementary, Dr. Watson. Simple, Inspector Lestrade."

So the "tattooed lady," whose mammary endowments are so fulsomely displayed in one of the figures in Dr. Goldstein's article, would be well-advised to stay in the shade—otherwise she will get the itch in what must be some uncomfortable locations not usually exposed to the sun and not originally designed for photosensitivity. Her "host," of course, will have to do the scratching and, for that and other reasons relating to the natural progression of romantic attachments, may want to part company with the "lady." For this purpose some of Dr. Goldstein's patients turned to the long-established and heroic method of dermabrasion. But a new method for getting rid of unwanted tattoos has been reported recently; this method makes use of the high-energy light beam, the laser. Although this use of the laser is still an investigative procedure requiring a specially designed laboratory and safety program, the results are promising in terms of removal of the tattoo with minimal scarring. So, sailors home from the sea (and other ports), take cheer over that sometimes embarrassing, and occasionally photosensitive, tattoo!

As for Sherlock Holmes, his creator, Dr. Arthur Conan Doyle, tells us that Holmes was a student and connoisseur of tattoos. As recounted in the story "The Gloria Scott," his very first case (while he was in college) turned on the clue of an unsuccessfully obliterated tattoo. And in "The Red-headed League" Holmes later revealed his expertise when he commented to his client, "The fish that you have tattoo'd immediately above your right wrist could only have been done in China. I have made a small study of tattoo marks and have even contributed to the literature of the subject. That trick of staining the fish's scales a delicate pink is quite peculiar to China." Clearly Sherlock Holmes knew his tattoos.

November, 1967

"Ye gads! I just got the over-all picture!"

13

Things That Go Bump in the Night

Man has a capacity for anxiety that is matched only by the plenitude of reasons for being anxious. As the old Cornish prayer says:

> From ghoulies and ghosties and long-leggity beasties
> And things that go bump in the night,
> Good Lord deliver us.

Well lots of people are having trouble sleeping these nights and it isn't because of ghosts or Santa Claus bumping down the chimney—it's the "over-all picture."

The "over-all" picture is compounded from the never-ending barrage of bad news relentlessly thrust upon us by systems of instant communication and the unique ability of the human mind to extrapolate the present into the future. In these days of the widening gap between technological power and human wisdom, the over-all picture can hardly be said to be cheering. The list of crises threatening human society and survival comes only too readily to mind: nuclear annihilation, wars and rumors of war, overpopulation, environmental pollution, poverty, racial conflict, violence and crime, ethnic unrest and political polarizations the world over. All these bode ill for the rising tide of human expectations—not to mention lesser and more immediate matters such as missing paychecks, bills for the mortgage, skyrocketing costs of medical care, and many another effect of an ailing economy. Who wouldn't be anxious?

Yet in this month of the festival of Christmas, the traditional season of good cheer, it does not seem unreasonable to look for a few bright spots or fragments of silver lining to soften the gloom. We may take comfort in the fact that more and more people, young and old, are awake and concerned rather than asleep and oblivious to the knocks in the motor and the bumps in the night. We should not forget that there is a large reservoir of ordinary people with good will, thoughtfulness for others, a sense of fair play and justice, and common civility—attributes that never make the headlines because they are good, rather than bad, news. But "good news" is what Christmas is all about—the good news that in this brutal world evolving from "long-leggity beasties" there is good that may overcome the evil, love that may overcome the hate, and humanity as well as inhumanity of man to man.

Such good news is probably hard to hear if you are impoverished and hungry, displaced and homeless, disadvantaged and frustrated, sick and suffering, as, alas, so many of our fellow human beings find themselves to be. This is one of the main reasons why people are unhappy with, and critical of, the political leaders whom they hold responsible for the all-too-obvious defects of today's society. Whether poor *Homo sapiens*, that wise-foolish, heroic-absurd creature limited by his traits inherited from "long-leggity beasties" has the time and ability to achieve a viable new order—is anything but certain. Will his emotions and prejudices allow his reason and spirit to prevail? This uncertainty is part of the overall picture, stimulated by things that go bump in the night. Maybe it is just the cat on the piano keys or the raccoon in the garbage can. But then again maybe it isn't. In fact, you can be sure that it isn't.

When you and I sit bolt upright worrying about the kind of world our children and grandchildren will find themselves in, it is helpful to turn to some well-tested sources of re-assurance. "Faith, hope, and charity," said St. Paul, elab-orating on the message brought by the Master whose birthday is about to be celebrated: for the mystic, faith that there is power in the Mystery beyond us on which we can draw for help; for the humanist and agnostic as well as for the mystic, hope that such help may be forthcoming to help us help our-selves; for all men, love and charity between man and man as an essential ingredient in the solutions of our problems—those all-too-real and ominous things that go bump in the night.

December, 1970

Lincoln Public Library

—Courtesy of the artist,
Harold D. Smith

Part II

(1987-1994)

14

The Nightingales

Lincoln Library's Lovely Lively Literary Ladies

Having cast the above alliterative lure, let us begin with a disclaimer. This account of the Friday Morning Book Discussion Group was solicited by the editor of the *Lincoln Review*—it was not the idea of the author. To have been such would have been presumptuous for two reasons: the author is a newcomer to Lincoln and he is the only member of "the other" sex who regularly attended the Book Group during this, the eighth, season. He was abashed, but not to the extent of declining the editor's invitation.

How come one lone male? Well, the Library's prospectus contained no sex discrimination clause and this male, because of his wife's prolonged illness, had time and need for intellectual stimulation, preferably in a cheerful social atmosphere. (He certainly got it!) One other man, a member's husband, came, but alas only twice. Another member's husband (a violinist in the Boston Symphony Orchestra) told me, in his wife's presence, that he wished he could attend; she promptly told him to stick to his violin; he promptly told me I was a male renegade. At one time one of the other members (Anita) called me a "Sweeney among the nightingales." My attempt to understand the tortuous meaning of T. S. Eliot's poem of that name left me in considerable doubt as to how complimentary a label that might be. In any case, "Sweeney" felt welcomed by the "nightingales."

In the Lincoln Library the Book Discussion Group was the responsibility of the Assistant Librarian, our Ellen. She has been the group's organizer, leader, and intellectual spark-plug. She it is who, once the group has chosen the subject for the year, surveys and orders the books, uncovers a wealth of literary background material, enkindles the discussion, and, with a firm hand in a very soft glove, keeps the ladies (and Sweeney) more or less on the rails while the verbal fur flies (a mixed metaphor, ladies, I know).

Who are these nightingales who are making the fur fly? Sitting around the big square table in the Tarbell Room, the roster of the Group is approximately as follows. Next to Ellen is Elizabeth (steadily knitting and periodically emitting calming shafts of light into any intellectual darkness); Frannie and Anita (whose joint quick wit and repartee belie their slight appearance of seniority); Mary (generally mending some article of clothing while at the same time shooting down some wilder flight of literary fancy emanating from the rest of the group); Barbara (who, usually bouncing in late and with the current book only half-read, asks what is its structure and wouldn't it be better as a play—which, of course, she would like to direct); Florence of keen analytic mind and compassionate heart who invariably concludes that socio-economic factors are at fault); and on—some twenty ladies in all, and each and every one contributing, from her own experience and intellectual background, cogent remarks, informed criticism, stimulating quips, and humorous sallies. All these are the lovely nightingales who sang in such a lively manner in the Library on two Friday mornings of every month.

And what was the singing about? The chosen subject this season was Russian literature, mainly of the 19th Century. We began with Turgenev's *Fathers and Sons*, worked our way through Dostoyevsky's *The Brothers Karamazov*, wallowed in Tolstoy's *Anna Karenina*, read Bielly's *St. Petersburg*, and supplemented our acquaintance with that city of the Bronze Horseman through Gogol's brilliant but complex short stories, "The Nose," "Nevsky Prospect," and "The Overcoat," as well as through several short stories by Chekhov. Two of the most extraordinary books were Bulgakov's *The Master and Margarita* and Gogol's *Dead Souls*. The former is a Russian version of Faust and the Devil—here not Mephistopheles but Woland the Professor (who has his own account of Pontius Pilate's role in the Crucifixion). The latter book, *Dead Souls*, is the story of major character Chichikov's chicanery in purchasing the ownership of serfs who had died after the most recent census, for the purpose of boosting his mortgage collateral—a shady maneuver that today would certainly qualify him for "arbitrageurship" on Wall Street or for "cronyship" in more than one administration in Washington.

Indeed, heartless bureaucracy was portrayed most vividly by Gogol in his story "The Overcoat": an impoverished minor civil servant, Akaky Akakyevich, finally acquires a desperately needed and highly prized new overcoat only to be mugged and have the coat stolen on the very first night that he wore it. The satire lies in poor Akaky's complete brush-off by the local policeman, the police commissioner, and finally the Very Important Person, the general, with the result for poor Akaky of hypothermia and fatal pneumonia. The denouement comes when Akaky's ghost suddenly confronts the general in his open carriage on his way to his mistress, seizes his overcoat, and so reduces the Very Important Person to a

mass of terrified humble jelly. And lest we think that bureaucracy ended with the Tzars, we also read Vladimir Voinovich's *Ivankiad*, a delightful satire on bureaucracy in the
USSR today, and Hedrick Smith's book *The Russians*, a cor-
roborating account from his years in Moscow as *The New York
Times* correspondent. Voinovich, since his exile to the West,
has written a novel of wildly hilarious satire on the Red Army
and the KGB, *The Life and Misadventures of Private Ivan Chon-
kin*. Voinovich is a modern Russian "E. B. White" plus a touch
of "Thurber."

In contrast to the absurdities of Soviet bureaucracy, we
came, in Nadezhda Mandelstam's memoir *Hope Against Hope*,
to the harsher restrictions of Stalin and the KGB. Her husband, Ossip Mandelstam, was a well-known poet among the
Moscow intellectuals of the 1920s and 1930s. In 1933 Mandelstam composed but never published, a poem in which two
lines were derogatory of Stalin: "All we hear is the Kremlin
mountaineer / The murderer and peasant slayer." Such was
the fear of poetry as potential political dynamite that the of-
fending poet and his wife were banished from Moscow; subsequently he alone was sent to a Siberian work camp where
he died. His surviving wife's account, written in the 1960s of
the rigors of their preliminary harassment and hounding by
the KGB is a vivid revelation of what such intellectuals had to
undergo in the Stalinist period.

Besides the subjects of bureaucracy and political re-
pression, what other categories of issues, problems, and character, did the Group explore in this rich and complex Russian
fictional forest? First, there was the perennial conflict between
conservative fathers and rebellious sons (and their radical
friends): in *Fathers and Sons*, father Nikolai Petrovich Kirsanov
versus son Arkady and his friend Bazarov (the new "scientific" and nihilistic "angry young man"); in *The Brothers Ka-
ramasov*, Fydor Pavlovich Karamazov, old reprobate and se-

ducer, versus his four sons; and in *St. Petersburg*, Apollon Apollonovich, senator and member of the Establishment, versus son Nikolai Apollonovich, whose radical friends maneuvered him into planting a bomb under his own old father (suspense!!). On this general subject Sweeney wielded his sole advantage over the nightingales: only he was a father; (as a well-intentioned male chauvinist, he suggested for next year the subject of "mothers and daughters").

A second subject, the relationships of husbands and wives, was thoroughly explored (generally to the detriment of the husband): Anna and her lover Vronsky versus her husband Alexy Alexandrovitch Karenin; Darya (Dolly) Alexandrova versus her husband Stepan Arkadyevitch Oblonsky (who was Anna's brother); and a country landowner Levin (Tolstoy's portrait of himself?) and his little wife Princess Kitty Shtcherbatsky. Because many biographical facts about each author's childhood and presumptions about his sex life had been presented by Ellen and some of the members of the group, a great deal of illuminating instant psychoanalysis, applying to both the authors and their fictional characters, was passed back and forth across the table.

Finally, the subject of religion played a significant part in this literature. Who can forget Ivan Karamazov's story to his brother, Alyosha, of the Grand Inquisitor who personifies all the cruel mistakes of the organized Christian Church over the centuries, or the contrasting picture of the pure Christianity of Alyosha's mentor and guru, Father Zossima? The present Soviet society officially may be non-religious, but who can doubt that the Russian people possess an intensely emotional, if not morbid, religious streak, then and now.

By this time the reader must be aware that pronunciation of the long Russian names with their patronymics was a hurdle over which the group had to leap. And many were the disputes over literary meaning, style, and usage in all the words. For arbitration, these arguments usually were referred to Ellen's "bible," Vladimir Nabokov's *Lectures on Russian Literature*. But Mr. Nabokov's opinions were not always accepted, there being a certain stubbornness in nightingalian points of view. None of us spoke Russian but we were greatly helped early on in the season by a Russian who was teaching literature at the local High School; he gave us a fascinating talk on the language and literature of Russia, especially *The Brothers Karamazov*. The whole Book Discussion Group—nightingales and Sweeney—certainly finished the year with clearer insights into the character of Russia and the Russians, past and present, with their intense love for "Mother Russia." Such understanding by Americans has never been more needed than it is right now.

If the previous seven seasons of the Book Discussion Group were all as much fun as this, the eighth, has been, this participant has missed a lot. For the next, the ninth,year, the Group has decided to study the development of the English novel in the eighteenth, nineteenth, and twentieth centuries. At least we will be spared all those long Russian names as well as the problems of translation. That the nightingales then will sing just as sweetly as they have this year, is the fervent hope of their

"Sweeney"

Lincoln, MA
July, 1987

FATHERS *VERSUS* SONS

"How you can decline to recognize principles and precepts passes my comprehension. What other basis for conduct in life have we got?"

"I've told you already, uncle, that we don't recognize any authorities," Arkady interposed.

"We base our conduct on what we recognize as useful," Bazarov went on. "In these days the most useful thing we can do is to repudiate—and so we repudiate."

"Everything?"

"Everything."

"What? Not only art, poetry . . . but also . . . I am afraid to say it . . ."

"Everything," Bazarov repeated with indescribable composure.

Pavel Petrovich stared at him. He had not expected this; while Arkady positively glowed with satisfaction.

"However, if I may say so," began Nikolai Petrovich, "you repudiate everything, or, to put it more precisely, you are destroying everything . . . But one must construct too, you know."

"That is not our affair . . . The ground must be cleared first." —Ivan Turgenev: *Fathers and Sons*, 1862, chapter 10.

15

Watching a Pair of Lesser White-Crested Birdwatchers

Watching birds in the dark at 3 a.m.? No, it's not impossible for a mind's eye that has been sufficiently stimulated. And last night the mind's eye of this male member of the above-mentioned pair was so stimulated by the events of yesterday.

The day for my wife Teresa and myself had begun with a morning of birding on the dike at Concord's Great Meadows (lovely pintails, green-winged teals, great blue herons, hordes of Canada geese). The afternoon was spent perusing again our small battered loose-leaf notebook containing lists of birds seen on many an outing and trip of the last 47 years. In the evening, at dinner with daughter and son-in-law, Gwyn discussed good places for birdwatching in Lincoln and Rob twitted us again about a long-past "sighting" of Harris's sparrow (an old family joke). And finally at bedtime T. and I were reading E.B.White's delightful essay "Mr. Forbush's Friends" in which he enthuses over Edward Howe Forbush and his monumental work *Birds of Massachusetts and Other New England States* and diagnoses Mr. Forbush's birdwatching as sheer ecstasy. Hence my nocturnal avian musings.

It is with some temerity that I write about birdwatching by such non-expert amateurs as ourselves, newly come to Lincoln. For Lincoln is the headquarters of the Massachusetts Audubon Society, the home of Drumlin Farm, and a community crowded with expert ornithologists including a disciple of Ludlow Griscom, the publisher of Roger Tory Peterson, and the dentist-ornithologist whose dental chair is a unique glass-enclosed observation post from which you, the patient, watch his birds while he watches your teeth—and reports on penguins. But for ourselves, birding has been, not a scientific pursuit, but just a good hobby that has given interest and pleasure to the comings and goings of our married life.

Our birdwatching began in the spring of 1941 when, as newly-weds and strangers in New Haven, Conn., we needed an outdoor hobby to pursue together. Someone gave us a copy of Peterson's recently new and helpfully explicit *A Field Guide to the Birds*. We started in a state of complete ornithological ignorance: T. could only claim a grandfather who in 1855 had discovered the nesting site of the pink-footed goose in Spitzbergen and a father who had collected birds' eggs—an enthusiasm acceptable in earlier days; I had had in primary school one too many "bird walks." So, on our first outing with binoculars and Peterson in hand, we sighted a bird that I brashly identified from Peterson as Harris's sparrow; T. thought it looked more like a chickadee—which of course it was. From that abysmal point onwards the only possible direction for our birdwatching was up. Harris's sparrow, a bird of the U.S. midwest, began it all and in the process became a perennial family joke.

Despite this shaky start we learned fairly rapidly. The next year, during a two-week camping trip by Indian Lake in the Adirondacks, we ran up a list of 75 birds that included a host of warblers (with and without wing bars), an Acadian chickadee, three Arctic three-toed woodpeckers, and—on the last evening—our first sighting of a black-crowned night heron. From then on we were hooked; birding became an added spice to every trip, short or long, as we looked out for identifiable feathered friends, old and new. Here are some of our more memorable encounters.

Arctic three-toed woodpeckers

In the salt marshes of New Jersey's Brigantine Refuge there was the white snow goose, at Bombay Hook on Delaware Bay the flashing black and white beauty of a large flock of avocets. From our sleeping bags in the open by Middle Saranac Lake in the Adirondacks we awoke to see two large pileated woodpeckers just above our heads. Camping with our children in the wilds of Wyoming, we were introduced to trumpeter swans on Emma Matilda Lake and to yellow-headed black birds along Pacific Creek. In the 1960's, Florida (the Keys, the Everglades, Sanibel) added a whole flock of new birds to our life list from anhingas through pelicans to woodstorks. Jamaica gave us the streamer-tailed hummingbird, and the rocky shores of Nova Scotia the black and white willet. In the lake-bestrewn wilderness of northern Minnesota we canoed alongside a family of loons with the little ones riding on their mother's back; the haunting cries of the loons took us back to earlier years in Maine and the Adirondacks. On a trip to North Carolina to assuage our worry over the late arrival of the invitations for our daughter's upcoming wedding, we were treated to the not-inappropriate sight of the courting dance of two great blue herons in the shallow waters of Lake Mattomuskeet.

Willet

Our family visits to the British Isles exposed us to a whole new world of seashore and inland birds. Along the coast of Pembrokeshire in Wales there were the gannets with their white wings tipped with black, flying over the sea off St. David's Head and the coal-black choughs with their red bills, diving down the black cliffs of Pwllderi from the purple heather above toward the gray seals on the rocks below. There were guillemots, puffins, and oyster catchers along the rugged coast of North Devon, the red-throated diver (British version of our North American loon) with its family on little Ghleann Loch in Ardnamurchan by Scotland's Western Isles, and from many an upland moor or lowland meadow came the lonely cry of the curlew.

Red-throated diver

In our recent home at the foot of the Malvern Hills in Herefordshire we had plenty of well-known avian Britishers in our garden and at our feeder. Our favorite denizens were the house martins who returned each year to their mud-built nest under the eave, That is, until the house sparrows pecked a larger opening and threw the martin fledglings out. This crisis was solved by the purchase and installation of a Dutch manufactured imitation martin nest made of concrete— impervious to sparrow peckings—and our martins came back again. Nothing was more lovely than the flashing swoop of the martin's quick flight curving down and up to their under-eave nest. We are told that they still are there.

From England periodic sorties onto the Continent from time to time provided us with further avian encounters. In France, the Camargue, the vast wetland of the Rhone delta on the Mediterranean coast, was highlighted by the brilliant blue red and yellow bee-eaters from Africa (not to be confused with the scarlet beef-eaters of the Tower of London). But surely our most vibrant avian encounter there was in the streets of Arles where a large flock of swifts noisily raced round and round the outside circumference of the Roman-built Arena— no doubt anticipating the periodic bull-running in the amphitheater inside. In Crete we saw the crested lark hopping among the early spring wild flowers in the ruins of Minoan Gournia. Beyond Greece and Crete we did not go, thus leaving the exotic birds of Africa, the Orient, and the Antipodes to more vigorous, expert, and compulsive birders than ourselves.

If not to the East, at least to the West we did go for a change from the gray skies and short days of the English winter. In southern Arizona the Sonoran desert and mountains gave us a whole set of new birds including Gambel's quail (with its fancy forward-curled head crest) and the road runner which, when running, looked like nothing so much as a belated commuter dashing wildly after his departing train. And on the South Rim of the Grand Canyon, T. spied a mountain chickadee (which she did not confuse with Harris's sparrow).

Not all encounters with birds were far from home. A personal and more emotionally-charged encounter took place many years ago in our home in Pennsylvania. One day there fell down our chimney into the fireplace, in a cloud of soot, a screech owl. On the day before, redecoration and repainting of the living room had been completed. Consternation— visions of sooty wings beating against the new curtains! Solution of the crisis—sidewise insertion of a long-handled saucepan pinning the owl to the firescreen, saucepan screen and owl then carried out the front door. Relief—new decorations saved! We prefer our birds outdoors.

Many an unusual encounter by many a birdwatcher has been reported in the past to Mr. Forbush who recorded them in his *Birds of Massachusetts.* E.B. White relished these choice bits of information and reproduced a great many of them in his before-mentioned essay, such as, for instance, the battle to a draw between a great horned owl and a blacksnake, or the large bullfrog with a barnswallow in his mouth. To the author of this essay one of the most amusing was the report from Miss Elizabeth Dickens on Block Island that she had seen a brown creeper climbing a cow's tail. Surely this is a prime example of either blind ignorance of impending danger or sheer avian bravado.

And what do you think was the subject of one of the last paragraphs of EBW's essay? None other than our first friend, Harris's sparrow! EB regrets that, due to the demise of Mr. Forbush, he cannot be recorded after Mr. Fred G. Floyd of Hingham, as the second sighter of Harris's sparrow in New England. And to think that I might have joined them as the third—except, alas, it was only a black-capped chickadee. So much for the ornithological strivings of this not-very-expert watcher of birds. Nevertheless, in our relaxed approach to birding over almost five decades, the two of us have had a lot of enjoyment from our feathered friends.

Now, old bald eagle, turn over and go back to sleep.

Lincoln, MA
January, 1989

Harry and Chick

16

Avalanche of Paper, Deluge of Words

Who does not suffer from that daily encounter with the excessive communication of today's world that occurs on opening the over-stuffed mail box? Bulging with unsolicited advertisements from local stores and supermarkets, requests for contributions to innumerable worthy causes, brochures holding out tempting material possessions or excursions abroad, fat annual reports of corporations to stockholders printed in color on outrageously expensive glossy paper, urgent requests for money to meet the insatiable needs of political candidates, notices of lost children (from as far away as California), publications containing useful news of church and ongoing local activities, journals and magazines that one actually has subscribed to, bills (of course),—the mail box only occasionally reveals in the heart of this avalanche of paper and deluge of words the welcome nugget of a truly personal letter from a cherished friend.

But how to cope with this avalanche, this deluge? How

do we dig out, stay afloat, reduce the whole mass to a manageable situation? In a word, how do we "winnow" the wheat from the chaff? And what do we do with the "wheat" when separated? How do we store it and—more to the point—how do we retrieve it? This might be thought to be an irrelevant question in this community abounding in personal computers and computer experts. But I am not so sure that it is.

The answers, of course, depend on many factors including the character, occupation, and interests of the person involved and on his or her particular stage in life. The stage in life is important. I write as a septuagenarian who faces the challenge of "winnowing" to get rid of things. But the person in middle life, raising a family and absorbed in a professional or business career, has need of a different kind of "winnowing" of the communication avalanche; to this I can, at least, provide some hindsight.

Some twenty years ago as an active physician, scientist, and medical editor, I wrote an editorial on this subject, entitled "Where Did I See That Paper?" (*Ann, Intern, Med.* 67: 459-460, 1967); I quote it here in part: "The doctor, faced with a plethora of medical journals, adopts at one time or another one of the following courses: [1] He immediately throws the journals out unread (short-term efficiency, postgraduate non-education, and hard on patients); [2] he lets the journals pile up until wife or secretary issues an ultimatum: 'Either they go or I go!'; [3] he reads the tables of contents and then throws the journals out (short-term assuagement of conscience that he is 'following' the medical literature); [4] he reads the entire contents of each journal (and is 3 years behind, gets nothing else done, and accumulates unpaid bills); [5] he reads some of the articles that particularly interest him (and then has the problem of how to store, and later retrieve, this new information). To this end he may merely depend on memory (fraught with uncertainty), bind the journals for his library (scholarly, but space-consuming), send for reprints (neat—if you can get them), xerox the article (if you have a copying machine available and can afford it), or rend the journals asunder and file the torn-out papers (if you have a system that tells you where to file them and—more importantly—where to find them again).

Your Editor wishes that he could speak of personal filing systems from a strong experience, But alas, I cannot. On each of my three desks (editorial office, hospital office, and study at home) the ragged piles—journals, papers, reprints, tear sheets, xerox copies, notes, and manila folders—wax and wane in size but never disappear. These repositories of erstwhile information are the despair of my wife and secretaries, but they can be, and are, used by myself with intuitive techniques of retrieval reminiscent of the pointing setter or the fine art of dowsing. But periodically there comes a moment of truth when such material must either be stored systematically or thrown out—if for no other reason than to keep the cleaning woman from quitting. In the end sheer mass defeats fallible memory and cultivated intuition.

Let tomorrow's answers of microfilms and computers come as soon as they may; for most of us today's answers lie in the written word, the manila folder, the index card, and the will to use them. Good storage and good hunting!"

Now, two decades later, most physicians and scientists, as well as the rest of the world, presumably are computerized completely and hence free of the problems of retrieval. So far so good, but even that miraculous storer of electronic bytes generates, from its companion printer, its own avalanche of paper (yards of it!) in the need to have words that can be read away from the screen of the monitor. Thus it is just possible that in this town, even today, there are desks buried under unorganized middens of accumulated print-outs as well as other papers, articles, clippings, photocopies etc., etc. And there even may be closets and basements stacked high with old magazines and journals awaiting disposal but secure in the natural procrastination of their owners. It is just such veritable squirrel's nests of papers and words—hoarded against the day of some vaguely anticipated possible use—that brings me to the different kind of "winnowing" that confronts those of us in the the later and decelerating phases of life.

This is the "winnowing down" process that stems from the axiomatic truth that "you can't take it with you." It usually occurs in successive stages; for example, my wife and I have gone through the following: [1] closing out the 3-storey house of our middle years and raising a family, [2] moving abroad to a 2-storey house in England to begin our retirement, [3] moving back to the U.S. and Lincoln to a 1-storey condominium with basement. With each move we have shed a lot of furniture and a few books, but most of the books and practically all the papers are still with us. And still ahead there lies yet a further move [4] to an even more restricted "life care" retirement home—what then?

Clearly, further and more drastic winnowing is in order. One must distill out the very essence of one's supportive possessions that have come to symbolize one's life—the "lares and penates" of one's successive homes. This is not easy. Books: we can't part with all our favorites yet for they surround us with the aura of a long-familiar world. (Pace, Friends of the Library with your monthly book-sales,—later, later). Interesting articles, amusing cartoons, inspiring clippings, old tax returns (held against a long-past possible audit): weed them out if you can and, at least, put the inevitably large residue into some kind of organized binders or files. Photographs and color slides: beware of this fascinating and totally time-consuming pastime that is better put off until one is less mobile. And old letters?

Letters constitute the major winnowing hurdle for they

evoke the spirits of cherished personalities from the near and distant past. Once immersed in these ghostly sheets of paper and words, it is almost impossible to surface, let alone to throw anything away. Here is my mother in a courtship letter to my father-to-be urging a bit more patience; here is my grandmother advocating the goal of making other people happy (and in the same breath advising my mother to get another ball of wool for her knitting). Here are the daily love-letters from our own courtship of nearly half a century ago (too poignant to read under present circumstances of old age—but don't part with them yet!). Here are letters from our children (daughter sleeping on the London pavement in front of St. Paul's in order to see the funeral of Sir Winston Churchill, son describing his first long canoe trip in the Canadian wilderness).

Here are innumerable letters from professional mentors and colleagues summoning up memories of many a medical venture, research project, gala occasion.

Some of the letters even recall long-forgotten incidents; for example, here is a letter from the editor of a medical journal in Chicago to whom we had submitted a manuscript on the dire physiological effects on castaways who succumb to drinking sea-water (World War II). He requests a duplicate copy of one of the main graphs because the original inadvertently had blown out of the window on the 18th floor and could not be found in the surrounding streets! (He got the copy, the paper was published, but whether it led to any saving of life I do not know).

So here are one's memories embedded in words on paper, one's "lares and penates," one's treasures that "moth and dust doth corrupt" and that cannot be taken with you to heaven or to wherever else you may or may not be going. As they cannot be entombed with you like a pharaoh in Egypt, or burned with you on a funeral pyre like a maharajah in India, you are left with three choices: [1] ruthlessly discard, burn, throw away, get rid of; [2] find some unwary and enthusiastic archivist in a medical, historical, or Quaker library who will receive and guard your treasures (and let time and the pressures on space lead to the ultimate disposal; [3] leave your treasures to be dealt with by your children. This latter choice will be a burden for them which it would be well to minimize as they already have their own homes filled to the ceilings with their own "lares and penates"—and you want them to remember you *lovingly*. Clearly now is the time to fish or cut bait, the time for decision and action, for sorting, eliminating, and organizing a small residue. But then, perhaps, it might be better to do it *next* winter.

Beware the avalanche, beware the deluge, for paper and words will pursue you to the end!

*   *   *

Postscript: That is, until all the forests are cut down, all the cellulose is gone, and the avalanche of paper thunders no more. But, as the earth's supply of silicates is practically inexhaustible, words will persist, embedded in the computer's silicon microchips—perhaps a case of the bark no longer being worse than the byte. Then the problem will be: what to do with all the disks—floppy or otherwise? In the words of that master wordsmith, the Bard of Avon, the bottom line still will be as in Hamlet's lament: "Words, words, words!"

May, 1988

17

From Crete to Arizona, Gathering Time

To everything there is a season, and a time
for every purpose under heaven:
                                    —*Ecclesiastes 3:1*

This winter, during Lent, while some of our friends and
neighbors were gathering personal and spiritual time, my
wife Teresa and I flew to southern Arizona to gather bits of
time ourselves. We returned with a mixed bag of times of several kinds: personal time. historical time, geology's deep time,
and even deeper cosmological time. Different kinds of time?
What do I mean?

Perhaps we can approach the subject by commenting on
the similarities and contrasts between two areas in the world
each of which we have visited on a number of occasions during the past dozen years, namely, the Aegean island of Crete
and the Sonoran Desert of southern Arizona. Both areas have
given us rich and memorable samples of these various kinds
of time.

The *personal times* of our pleasure and stimulation in these new and different places were measured only in days or a few weeks out of the allotted years of our personal lives. Our two trips to Crete showed us the long snow-capped mountain ranges that form the central spine of the island, the arid hillsides and olive groves, the black-robed peasant women working beside their fagot-bearing donkeys, and their men sitting around the tavernas in the village squares. This was the Crete of today.

Historical time in Crete was revealed by the great archaeological sites and finds of the ancient Minoan civilization. This historical time stretched over four thousand years: Minoan Crete from 2000 B.C. to its sudden collapse about 1400 B.C., domination by the Mycenaean and the Dorian Greeks, subsequent waves of conquest by Venetians, Turks, and even Germans (briefly, in World War II) . The most intriguing reminders of the ancient past were the Minoan palace buildings at Knossos which were discovered, excavated, and partially restored by Sir Arthur Evans early in this century; many of the bright wall-paintings and gold and bronze artifacts are exhibited in the nearby museum in Herakleion. All these sights tell us of the home of King Minos, of the legendary labyrinth of the Minotaur, and of the mythological saga of Theseus' rescue, with the aid of Princess Ariadne, of the enslaved Athenian youths from the horns of the bulls—a story vividly told by Mary Renault in her novel *The King Must Die.*

The *personal times* of our three trips to southern Arizona also were measured in a few weeks each. From the town of Green Valley, lying between Tucson and the Mexican border, we explored the desert, its mountain ranges, and its birdlife. In Madera Canyon at the foot of the twin peaks of the Santa Rita Mountains we saw many new birds, including hummingbirds, painted redstarts, bridled titmice, acorn woodpeckers, and in the desert, phainopeplas, Gambel's quails, roadrunners, and many another. We visited Cave Creek Canyon in the Chiricahua Mountains (last stronghold of the Apaches), and approached the canyon at the foot of Baboquivari Peak (where "Jonnie"Fisk netted birds for banding and subsequently wrote *The Peacocks of Baboquivari.*)

What of *historical time* in Arizona? In the white mission church of San Xavier del Bac, founded by Jesuit Padre Kino in 1700 and still in use, and the unfinished mission church of the Franciscans at Tumacacori, we saw tangible signs of the Spanish military and religious invasion of Mexico and the Southwest that antedated the coming of the Americans (to get the full flavor of that time read Willa Cather's *Death Comes to the Archbishop.*) And on the reservations the black-haired and dark-skinned Papagos and Pima Indians reminded us of the indigenous inhabitants of these lands over prehistoric and historic times. These ranged from the Incas of Peru through the Mayans and Aztecs of the Yucatan to the Indians of Mexico and the Pueblo peoples who were the precursors of the present-day Hopi and Navahos of Arizona and New Mexico. This time-span of a millennium and a half is a shorter sample of historical time than that from Crete but is similar in the violent rises and falls of peoples and cultures.

But what about *deep time*, deep geological time? And how did we glimpse it as well in Crete and Arizona? In his very readable book on the geological formation of the North American continent, *Basin and Range* (1980), John McPhee coined the term "deep time" for the time span of 4.6 billion, or 4600 million, years of the existence of the planet Earth. Such deep time is measured in units, not of centuries (100 years) nor of millennia (1000 years), but of "megacenturies" (100 million years). As we flew over the mountains of Crete and the ranges and desert basins of Arizona and considered how they came to be, we had to dive—or at least belly-flop—into the newly accepted theory of plate tectonics and continental drift.

The plate tectonic theory, supported by evidence such as the volcanic activity of the mid-Atlantic and mid-Pacific ridges, directional magnetism of rocks, and the similarities of widely separated floras and faunas, holds that the continents are the upper parts of a series of crustal plates that float on the heavier mantle encasing the Earth's molten core, plates that move about over the surface of the globe. At rates of a few centimeters per year, such peregrinations require the deep time of many millions of years.

When two plates collide, one plate subducts at an angle under the other, the rocks in the mantle become molten magmas that lead to volcanoes and earthquakes behind the mountains piling up on the overriding plate. When plates separate, oceans are formed; when plates bulge upward, the sedimentary rocks formed under shallow seas become high plateaus or mountains. Given deep time, the surface of the globe is indeed a restless place.

What has been the itinerary of these restless continents in their wanderings during "recent" deep time? Well, between 270 and 225 million years ago most of the continental plates seem to have collided with each other to form a supercontinent, now named Pangaea; then 180 million years ago the Americas began to separate off and the Atlantic Ocean came into being. Beginning 50 million years ago the India plate collided with Asia and crumpled up the Himalayas, and Africa, driving against Europe, produced the Alps and the Mediterranean volcanoes.

So, when we went to Crete we met deep time as well as historical time. As we flew from Athens to Herakleion, we passed over the semi-circular island and steep cliffs of Santorini; this is the caldera, or all that is left, of the great volcano of Thera that exploded in about 1450 B.C. and must have contributed to the collapse of the Minoan civilization on Crete. From this great cataclysmic event probably originated, via the

Egyptians, Plato's legendary story of the sudden sinking of Atlantis into the sea. And as we approached Crete, 70 miles on across the open sea, we saw the long east-west line of the island's mountains, a line which parallels the coast of Egypt lying across the Mediterranean to the south. Here again we glimpse deep time as we visualize the Aegean plate over-riding the oncoming African plate with the crumpling up of the Cretan mountains and the heating up of the volcano behind them—a process that began many millions of years ago.

What of *deep time* in Arizona? Flying on from Denver to Tucson, we became aware of the predominantly north-south orientation of mountain ranges and the wide flat areas or basins that lie between them. This is the "basin and range" country of Utah, Nevada, and southern Arizona, where mountains have been formed by a different mechanism. Here the continent is stretching in an east-west direction and, as it has done so over a few million years, cracks or faults have loosened up great blocks of the continental crust. These blocks began to tilt, the upper sides became the ranges, the lower sides, filling with rocks and sand eroding from the ranges, became the basins. As we stood among the towering saguaros west of Tucson and gazed southward toward the Mexican border, the wide desert basin was rimmed on the east by the Sierrita and the Santa Rita Mountains and on the west by the

Baboquivari Range with its dramatic monolithic Peak in the middle and Kitt Peak on the near end. Could we see the ranges tilting upward and the desert tilting downward and the sea creeping in? Not quite—the process was just a little too slow. Rationally we knew that deep time was there but could we really comprehend it?

Here we humans are, living in the 70 to 80 years of personal time, aware of a family time perhaps of 5 generations spanning some 150 to 200 years, learned in historical time of 4000 to 5000 years, but faced with a time scale of an entirely different order of magnitude: the deep geological time of hundreds of millions or billions of years. Our only hope of gaining some degree of comprehension of such deep time and its relation to personal time is to resort to analogy and metaphor. To this end, let us turn to my 7-foot high great-great-great-grandfather's clock, encased in polished cherry wood, which makes one loud tick each second. If each tick were equivalent to one year's time, then 150 years ago would be equivalent approximately to the beginning of the Earth and the subsequent 4,730,400,000 ticks would equal the 4.7 billion years of the Earth's age. Then 105 years ago life began, 14 years ago life came ashore, 2 years ago the dinosaurs became extinct and the mammals took over, 3 1/2 days ago *Homo sapiens* evolved, 70 minutes ago history began, 33 minutes ago Christ was born, 4 minutes ago the age of science and the Industrial Revolution began, and only 89 seconds ago the 20th century began. Although this perspective on deep time has been "gathered" in our own living room at home, it helps us to understand why we couldn't quite see the basins and ranges tilting in Arizona.

Even deep geological time is not quite the limit to our gathering of time in Arizona. The white domes of the National Observatory on Kitt Peak in the Baboquivaris, and the tiny Smithsonian Observatory on Mt. Hopkins in the Santa Ritas, remind us that there is a still deeper time —*cosmological time*. As the telescopes reach out to the galaxies and quasars 8 to 10 billion light-years away, mankind is seeing parts of the early universe as they were soon after the Big Bang perhaps some 15 billion years ago. Was that the beginning of time? Stephen Hawking, astrophysicist, cosmologist, and present-day successor to Newton and Einstein, has wrestled with this problem in his recent book, *A Brief History of Time*, (1988). Hawking combines the 4-dimensional space-time of Einstein 's theory of general relativity with quantum mechanics to conclude "that space and time together might form a finite, four-dimensional space without singularities or boundaries, like the surface of the earth but with more dimensions". That is, using the earth as a model, if space and time start with the Big Bang at the North Pole and expand to the Equator, they then contract toward the Big Crunch at the South Pole where they go on to expand again. Such would be space and time without beginning or end.

This model of Hawking's encapsulates completely the basic dichotomy in the nature of time, namely, that between time going somewhere—time's arrow—and time going around again and again—time's cycle; this is the dichotomy that Stephen Jay Gould has presented so cogently in his book, *Time's Arrow, Time's Cycle: Myth and Metaphor in the Discovery of Geological Time*, (1987). Continental plates move forward and back again, mountains rise up and erode down and rise up again, the universe expands and contracts and expands again. Is it, and are we, going anywhere? Can we distinguish the past from the future? Hawking says that there are three arrows of time that do make this distinction: the thermo-dynamic arrow, the direction of time in which disorder in-creases; "the psychological arrow, the direction of time in which we remember the past and not the future; and the cos-mological arrow, the direction of time in which the universe expands rather than contracts". He believes that "intelligent beings can exist only in the expanding phase" because only it has a strong thermodynamic arrow. In other words, our time's arrow is riding only the forward-running part of one cycle of a time that has no beginning and no end. Time such as that is the deepest time of all—*eternity*.

The arrow of our musings has arrived at the bottom line, at the Great Mystery: *why* is the universe cycling through time to eternity? And what is the meaning of it all for the human species that has arrived so very recently and so very very ex-plosively on this infinitesimally small portion of it? Is there a Power, or God, behind and within this ongoing creation? Is it a Power that the human mind and soul can tap? The answer in the Christian message of Lent and Easter is "yes "; in the midst of evil, suffering, and death, there is hope and love and life. This is the *timelessness* that may be gathered by us all.

> A time to be born, and a time to die...
> A time to weep, and a time to laugh...
> A time to cast away stones, and a time to gather
>   stones together...

Lincoln, MA
June, 1989

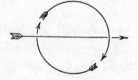

COSMOLOGICAL TIME

Before 1915, space and time were thought of as a fixed arena in which events took place but which was not affected by what happened in it. The situation is quite different in the general theory of relativity. Space and time are now dynamic quantities. . .The old idea of an essentially unchanging universe that could have existed, and could continue to exist, forever [is] replaced by the notion of a dynamic, expending universe that seems to have begun a finite time ago and might end a finite time in the future. —Stephen Hawking, *A Brief History of Time* (1988).

PERSONAL TIME

That's how fast it all happened as the years clicked past. One day I stood at the altar, young and unhappy about the prospect of living happily ever after. The next I was walking around the block with granddaughters. It had all gone by so fast, and my wife and I were living in a new world governed by people whose diapers we used to change. — Russell Baker, *There's a Country in My Cellar* (1990).

Dr. James Hutton

Fig. 1.   Father of Deep Geological Time

18

Doctors Far Afield

On the occasion of the 50th reunion of our Class of 1937 at Harvard Medical School, perusal of the reunion biographies of the surviving members revealed a wide variety of extra-medical activities, hobbies, and interests. These included traveling, sports, gardening, painting, flying light airplanes, doing archeology in the Andes, and even growing pecans in the remoter—from Harvard—area of southern New Mexico. Such activities may have been carried on during our active professional lives or after our retirement, or both. But they indicate that our interests and capabilities were not confined to the exacting medical domain of Aesculapius.

That medical men have distinguished themselves in careers in fields beyond those of the healing arts and sciences, is a long-known and well-recognized fact. All of us can reel off the names of many famous authors and writers who had been trained in medicine, names such as Somerset Maugham, Arthur Conan Doyle, Anton Chekov, Oliver Wendell Holmes, S. Weir Mitchell, Wilder Penfield, and our own inimitable Lewis Thomas. Medical poets, of course, include John Keats, Robert Bridges (Poet-Laureate of England), Oliver St. John Gogarty,

William Carlos Williams, and—closer to our Harvard Medical home—Hans Zinsser and Merrill Moore. In the field of botany physicians long have distinguished themselves, probably because of their interest in the healing properties of plants: Carolus Linnaeus of Sweden (father of botanical taxonomy), John Fothergill of London, William Withering of Birmingham, Joseph Leidy of Philadelphia. Examples of physicians as non-medical scholars are William James, philosopher, and Albert Schweitzer, organist, authority on the music of Bach, and Biblical scholar as well. And in the more vigorous and physically demanding fields of exploration and mountaineering we have—especially—Edward Adrian Wilson, physician, naturalist, artist, who with Scott in 1912 lost his life on the return journey from the South Pole. In the Arctic there is Elisha Kent Kane and Frederick Albert Cook of less admirable repute. Among the mountaineers there immediately comes to mind our medical contemporary from Columbia, Charles Houston, who led two of the assaults on the second highest mountain in the world, K-2 in the Karakoram.

Joseph Garland, when he was Editor of the *New England Journal of Medicine*, recognized the interest inherent in such non-medical achievements by physicians and surgeons and, in the 1960s, introduced a feature entitled "Doctors Afield", a feature which was carried on by his successor, Franz Ingelfinger. There we read about such medical men as Stephen Wooten Bushell who became the leading expert on Chinese ceramics, Ernesto (Che) Guevara, the Cuban and Latin American revolutionary and idol, and a series of other medicos whose activities were far afield from those of the caduseus and gold-headed cane.

Having painted, with a broad and shallow brush, this picture of doctors far afield from their medical careers, I thought that I might tell you briefly of four such men with whom you may not be so familiar. These are interesting and unusual characters, trained in medicine, whom I have come across during my retirement while puttering around in the minor byways of medical history. I give you a pioneer geologist, a student of the physics of light and decoder of Egyptian hieroglyphics, an amateur architect who designed one of America's foremost buildings, and a famous Himalayan mountaineer.

JAMES HUTTON (1726-1797), (Figure 1), was an 18th Century Scotsman who studied medicine at Edinburgh and Leyden and came back to practise in his native city of Edinburgh. But finding the competition of already-established medical practitioners to be too formidable, he withdrew to the farm which he had inherited and took up scientific farming. In this pursuit he became very much interested in the qualities and chemical compositions of different soils and began to ponder their origins.

Hutton lived at a time when the age of the Earth generally was believed, on Biblical evidence, to be some 6000 years old and the rocks of the Earth's surface to be entirely the result of sedimentation and compression in Noah's great flood (so-called "Neptunism"). Yet he saw the effects of water eroding and washing down the uplands and he observed, near Edinburgh and on the Scottish coast, rocks of volcanic origin— igneous basalts and metamorphosed rocks such as granite and schists—which intruded into sedimentary formations. Hutton concluded that the land had been formed by volcanic uplift due to heat in the interior of the earth and by the subsequent wearing down of the mountains by water to form sediments under the seas. He theorized that this was a repetitive or cyclic process, a process that is endless. "We find", he wrote, "no vestige of a beginning, no prospect of an end". The purpose of this mechanism, he believed, was to make the Earth permanently inhabitable for all forms of life and especially for humankind. The title of the book in which he presented his con-

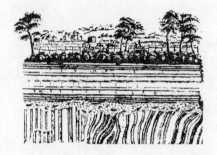

Fig 2.　Unconformity near Jedburgh, Scotland

Celebrated schematic engraving by John Clark of Eldin in
James Hutton's book *Theory of the Earth*, 1795.

Fig. 3　Unconformity at Siccar Point on the Scottish
　　　North Sea coast east of Edinburgh

Late Devonian sandstone (350 million years old)
　　overlying vertical Silurian shales (400 million years
　　old).

Modern photograph by Henry Faul, from *It Began with a
　　Stone* by Henry and Carol Faul, John Wiley & Sons,
　　New York; 1983.

cept was descriptive: "Theory of the Earth, an Investigation of the Laws Observable in the Composition, Dissolution, and Restoration of Land Upon the Globe".

But Hutton realized that the process he was proposing required time, an enormous amount of time, time of an entirely different order of magnitude. To support this concept he sought, and found, evidence in the record of the rocks. He discovered and described a number of so-called "angular unconformities" in which relatively level sedimentary rocks overlay such rocks that were tilted vertically, (Figure 2). The most striking of these unconformities was found exposed by the sea at Siccar Point on the Scottish North Sea coast, east of Edinburgh, (Figure 3). When Hutton showed this unconformity to several of his younger associates, one of them, John Playfair, later wrote, "On those of us who saw these phenomena for the first time...What clearer evidence could we have had of the different formation of these rocks, and of the long interval which separated their formation...The mind seemed to grow giddy by looking so far into the abyss of time." Thus James Hutton is credited with being the discoverer of "deep" geological time and hence is widely considered to be the "father of modern geology". And as such he was an essential forerunner to Charles Darwin whose theory of evolution by natural selection required time—lots and lots of time. Not bad for a physician whose medical career was nipped in the bud.

James Hutton was a likeable, vivacious—even impulsive—man who was part of the intellectual elite of 18th Century Edinburgh. His friends included men such as Adam Smith, David Hume, and James Watt. Joseph Black, professor of chemistry, had originally stimulated Hutton's interest in that field (from which he progressed on to medicine). John Playfair, professor of mathematics, was his intimate friend and later his expositer and biographer. Hutton was elected to the Royal Society of Edinburgh in 1785.

This amiable and versatile erstwhile physician, James Hutton, swam into my ken a few years ago when my wife and I were on a short trip to southern Arizona. In an effort to catch up on the modern theory of plate tectonics and continental drift as applicable to understanding the Western landscape, I was reading John McPhee's delightful book, *Basin and Range*, and Stephen Jay Gould's *Time's Arrow, Time's Cycle*. Both these books tell the story of James Hutton and both reproduce the famous drawing from Hutton's book illustrating the angular unconformities that substantiated beyond doubt his concept of deep geological time.

The remaining three examples of "doctors far afield" I ran across as I was co-authoring a little book on interesting Quaker doctors who were to be found in the 300-year history of the Society of Friends. One of these was Dr. Thomas Young of London.

THOMAS YOUNG (1773-1829), (Figure 4), born into a Quaker family in Somerset, England, was a child prodigy who taught himself more than a dozen classical, modern, and oriental languages. As an adult he studied medicine, made basic contributions to physiological optics and physics, and was said to be the most highly educated physician of his day.

Young studied medicine in London, Edinburgh, and Gottingen where he received his MD in 1796, with another MD from Cambridge in 1808. From 1799 to 1814 he practised medicine in London—a practice that was reported to be not too successful because "he studied symptoms too closely, but his treatments were successful". He taught at Middlesex Hospital and served as Physician to St. George's Hospital. He became a pioneer in the field of ophthalmology, being the first to describe the physiology of accomodation, astigmatism, and color blindness. For these scientific contributions he was elected to the Royal Society. His interest in optics led him to promulgate

Fig. 4   Dr. Thomas Young

Courtesy of the New York
    Public Library

Fig. 5   The Rosetta Stone

Courtesy of the British Museum

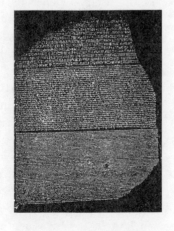

the undulatory or wave-like nature of light, as well as theories of mechanics and energy; in these he was a forerunner of modern physics.

Young's interests and achievements as a "natural philosopher" resulted in his appointment to a number of administrative posts in the field of science. He became foreign secretary of the Royal Society, secretary to the Royal Commission on Weights and Measures, and consultant to the Admiralty where he standardized longitude and theorized on the mechanism of the tides.

Perhaps Young's most famous non-medical achievement was as a philologist when he began the successful deciphering of the Rosetta Stone (in the British Museum), (Figure 5), to provide the key to Egyptian hieroglyphics, a process that was completed later by the French scholar Champollion. Thus Dr.Young added Egyptology to his already well-filled quiver; he wrote the article on Egypt in the *Encyclopedia Britannica* edition of his time.

What manner of man was this paragon who happened also to be a physician? He was said to be a tall handsome man, kind, unselfish, generous, and happy—a man fond of society. He was a singer, flutist, and dancer, and an excellent horseman. Thomas Young was indeed a man of genius and tremendous versatility, a "man of all seasons".

WILLIAM THORNTON (1761-1828), (Figure 6), a contemporary of Thomas Young, likewise was a physician who became notable for activities outside the field of medicine, in his case, as an inventor and an architect.

Thornton was born into a Quaker family on Tortola, in the British Virgin Islands, and was sent to England at an early age. He became the protege of the eminent Quaker physician in London, Dr. John Coakley Lettsom (who also had been born on Tortola), and was sent to study medicine in Edinburgh. In

1797, with his MD degree, he returned to the United States and settled in Philadelphia to practise medicine—with what success it is not clear. He is known to have opposed Dr. Benjamin Rush's treatment of yellow fever with purging and bleeding, as well as to have disagreed, on the basis of his own experience on Tortola, with Rush's theory of the non-infectious origin of the disease.

Perhaps this opposition contributed to Dr. Thornton's evident spare time, time which he devoted to other activities. For example, he became an inventor and was associated with John Fitch in producing several steamboats operated by paddlewheels which ran successfully on the Delaware River (well before Robert Fulton ran his more-celebrated steamboat on the Hudson). And then Thornton dabbled in amateur architecture. With no architectural experience whatever he entered, at the request of Benjamin Franklin, the competition for the design for the new first Public Library in Philadelphia. With his "plan on the ancient Ionic order", as he put it, he won; the resultant building was considered to be one of the finest in the country at that time and stood until 1880.

In 1790, on the advice of his mentor in London, Dr. Lettsom, Dr. Thornton and his newly married and very young bride moved back to Tortola where greater demand for his medical services might allow him to make a little more money. Two years later, having found the climate to be enervating and unhealthy, they returned to Philadelphia. While still in Tortola, Thornton had heard of a competition for a design of the new Capitol to be built in the proposed new capital city on the shores of the Potomac and he drew up a set of plans. On arrival in Philadelphia he was told that the competition was closed but that President Washington and Secretary of State Jefferson were not satisfied with the submissions. Dr. Thornton immediately obtained an introduction to the President, presented his design, and it was accepted, (Figure 7). Thornton

Fig. 6   Dr. William Thornton

Courtesy of the Corcoran
Gallery of Art

Fig. 7 Dr. Thornton's winning drawing in the
competition for the design of the Capitol

The present high dome of the Capitol was added some
fifty years later.

The original drawoing is in the Library of Congress.

became quite a close intimate of President Washington and was appointed as one of the three commissioners of the new city of Washington.

Thus Dr. Thornton gave up his medical career and moved to Washington. Later, in 1802, he became the first Commissioner of Patents (where he filed eight patents of his own over the next 25 years). During the war of 1812 he served as an officer in the Militia that opposed the British during the sacking of Washington. He was a magistrate and in later years he acquired a farm in Maryland where he bred race horses (a far cry from his Quaker origin). His skills and accomplishments as an artist and as a humanitarian were many: he painted, he drew, he wrote a treatise on teaching the deaf and dumb to speak, he strove to free slaves through recolonization in Africa.

Here we have another "man of all seasons" spreading well beyond the confines of the medical profession. On his death he was eulogized as "a scholar and gentleman—full of talent and eccentricity—a man of infinite humour—humane and generous...his company was a complete antidote to dullness". And not bad to have as his memorial the Capitol of the United States.

T. HOWARD SOMERVELL (1890-1975). For the fourth and last of my "doctors far afield" let us come forward to the 20th Century and turn to a surgeon, a man who, before the start of his medical career, achieved fame as a great mountaineer, (Figure 8).

Howard Somervell was born in Kendal in the English Lake District. At an early age he began to climb mountains, first in England and Wales, then in the Alps, and so became a highly skilled mountaineer. He attended Cambridge University (where he achieved high honors) and went on to study medicine at University College Hospital, London, where he received his MB and BCh in 1921.

In that year British climbers in Tibet were reconnoitering the northern approaches to Mt. Everest as a prelude to the first attempt to climb the mountain the following year. For that attempt Somervell was chosen to join the team of skilled climbers set to assault the summit. In this capacity he participated in the famous British Everest Expeditions of 1922 and 1924..

On the first expedition of 1922 successive camps were established on the mountain but, due to extreme cold, storms, and lack of oxygen, Somervell, Mallory, and their companions in a series of attempts were unable to get higher than to within half a mile below the summit. Then disaster hit in the form of a massive avalanche: Mallory, Somervell, and Crawford survived and rescued a few of the Sherpa porters but seven of the porters were lost.

Two years later Mallory with Somervell and others returned to try again. During preliminary climbing to establish camps on the North Col and on the ridge to the summit, Somervell performed a feat of extraordinary courage and skill for which he received great acclaim. Following a severe blizzard four of the porters were stranded, too frightened to move, on a steep slope of loose snow just above the lip of a great crevasse; Somervell with Mallory and Norton set out to rescue them. Somervell on the end of the fully extended rope found himself some ten yards short of the terrified men. Untying himself from the safety of the rope, he edged with great skill and care across the slope and led the men one by one back to safety; two of them he hauled by the collar from the very brink of the abyss. All survived—including Somervell.

Subsequently the highest camp was established on the side of the ridge just below the summit pyramid and the final assaults were begun. The first try by Mallory and Bruce was defeated by the zero cold and wind. Somervell and Norton made the second attempt.

Fig. 8   Mr. T. Howard Somervell

On Mt. Everest in 1924

Reproduced from *Fight for Everset,*
1924 by E. R. Norton, Longman,
Green & Co. New York, 1925.

Fig. 9   On Mr. Everest in 1924
within a thousand feet of
the summit

Photo taken by Somervell after
his collapse, showing
Norton striving to climb a
little higher.

Reproduced from *The Story of*
Everest by John Noel, Little,
Brown & Col, New York,
1927.

Without oxygen and in the poorly weather-proofed clothing of the time, they labored upward. Somervell's breathing and bronchial coughing with bleeding finally became so severe and painful that he collapsed; Norton went on a little further until, within a thousand feet of the top, he too collapsed, (Figure 9). Somehow the two climbers, confused and weakened from lack of oxygen, and Norton snow-blinded, managed to stumble back down to the safety of the camp.

Next day Mallory and Irvine started up, this time equipped with oxygen. They were last seen on the ridge just below the top pinnacle. They never returned. Whether they actually reached the summit before they fell to their deaths, is unknown. The tragedy ended the 1924 Expedition and the mystery remains, (Figure 10). It was 29 years—to 1953—before two men, Edmund Hillary and Sherpa Tenzing, stood on the top of Everest and returned to tell the tale.

As for our heroic surgeon, Howard Somervell, he took

Fig. 10   Members of the British Everest Expedition of 1924 (after the loss of Mallory and Irvine)

Somervell in back row, center.

Reproduced from Norton's book.

up his surgical career. Between the two Everest expeditions he had seen, and been appalled by, the suffering and misery of the peoples of rural India. So he volunteered to serve in, and subsequently became the head of, the London Missionary Society's Neypoor hospitals in Travancore in southern India. There he and his colleagues saw each year some 200,000 cases and performed 15,000 operations (he specialized in abdominal surgery). The growth of the Medical Mission was said to be a monument to Howard Somervell's Christian faith and leadership. After 21 years in India he retired to England in1945.

Howard Somervell was an artist—he painted especially in watercolor—and was a musician; he was brilliantly witty and a great lover of books. As stated in *The Times* obituary, his "ability as a mountaineer lay in his great strength (he once climbed 32 Alpine peaks in a six weeks' holiday) and in his poise, and he thought of mountaineering as a peerless expression of all the arts he practised"—including the art of healing.

* * *

These then are four more doctors of medicine who have made outstanding achievements outside the realm of medicine. How much their training in medicine contributed to success in their second careers, it is impossible to say. One took up his non-medical activities immediately after his training and never embarked on a medical career, one did so between his training and a subsequent long and active life in surgery, and two did so after a period in clinical practice. In any case they have added luster to our profession, luster not only for what they achieved but for the quality of men that they were. Whether judged to be geniuses or eccentrics, or both, our profession should be proud of them.

Bedford, MA
June, 1992

spirochetes Bacteria viruses sulphanilamide Penicillin Isoniazid

19

The Rise and Decline of the Age of Antibiotics

The Ongoing Contest Between Microbes and Mankind

Early in this 20th Century a new factor entered into the age-old contest between microbes and mankind. This was the extraordinarily successful transformation in the treatment of infectious diseases due to the discovery and development of specific antibiotics. From the perspective of my own 60 years in medicine let me tell you a few stories about their arrival.

In the autumn of 1936 the first specific antibiotic drug from Europe arrived at the Massachusetts General Hospital. It was sulfanilamide, or Prontosil, a sulfonamide that had been developed in the dye industry in Germany and had been found to be effective against the pathogenic gram-positive bacilli, the streptococci. Early in October of that year two young men were admitted at the same time to the MGH with identical acute streptococcal infections of the maxillary sinus—an ideal condition on which to test the new drug. One of these patients was a Harvard undergraduate who happened to be a son of the President of the United States, the other was a fourth-year student at Harvard Medical School, namely myself. Which of these two patients received the limited supply of this first new antibiotic drug, is not difficult to guess. Franklin Roosevelt, Jr., was back on the campus in Cambridge in a few days. I, who perhaps could be looked upon as a control having to rely on his own immune system, took a week or ten days to recover.

A more dramatic demonstration of the efficacy of the new antibiotic sulfonamides came my way the following year—late 1937 or early 1938—when I was an intern at the Pennsylvania Hospital in Philadelphia. One day 14 boys from a nearby reformatory were brought in with acute meningococcal meningitis, a disease with an expected mortality rate of 90 to 100 per cent. The Hospital had just received its first supply of a sulfonamide antibiotic from England. This new drug was used immediately to treat these fatally ill boys and, to our astonishment, 13 of the 14 recovered!

The sulfonamides, of course, were only the beginning; what of other infections for which they were not effective? Pneumococcal pneumonia had to wait for penicillin which became available some years later during World War II. The treatment of pneumonia at the time of my internship consisted of injections of the antiserum specific for one of the twenty-nine or thirty subtypes of pneumococci. Many a long night as a junior intern did I spend huddled over a microscope trying to determine which particular pneumococcal subtype was invading each of my patients on the ward and therefore which type of antiserum each required. But penicillin finally did arrive and with it the age of antibiotics was fully launched.

Tuberculosis was another major infectious disease whose treatment was revolutionized. Heretofore, this great scourge had been combatted only by public health measures to reduce exposure to very infectious "open cases" and by prolonged isolation and rest in sanatoria. Open cases of tuberculosis arriving in our general hospital were isolated and were much feared as "tb" was a high risk to doctors, nurses, and medical students—a risk to which not a few succumbed. However, all that was changed when, in the late 1940' s, antibiotics effective against the tubercle bacillus were discovered, first streptomycin and then isoniazid. Sanatoria were closed, artificial pneumothorax and surgical excision of infected lobes of lungs became treatments of the past, and this devastating infectious disease was assumed to be on the way to elimination.

So, during the 1930s and 1940s, began the age of antibiotics. Over the next quarter century many new and effective antimicrobial and antifungal drugs were discovered—to the great benefit of millions of patients (not to mention to the profits of competing pharmaceutical companies). It is true that in developing and exploring the use of these agents many undesirable side-effects were uncovered. However, over the years physicians and patients alike have come to believe that the discovery and use of antibiotic drugs, added to vaccination and other public health measures such as improved nutrition, hygiene, and sanitation, have obliterated infectious disease as a major threat to the human race. In a word, we have become complacent.

And now we are finding that this complacency is premature. The age of antibiotics, if not coming to an end, at least is entering a new stage, a stage characterized by the resurgence of old infectious diseases and the arrival of new ones. These challenges are due mainly to two factors: 1) development by pathogenic organisms of genetic resistance to

antibiotic drugs that formerly were effective, and 2) the oc-
currence of many social, demographic, and environmental
changes that promote the resurgence of old diseases and permit the emergence of new infectious organisms, mainly viruses.

The development of resistance to antibiotic drugs by
pathogenic microbes has been increasing rapidly during the
past five to ten years. That of the tubercle bacillus is perhaps
the most dramatic and alarming; more and more open cases
are appearing that are resistant to antibiotic therapy. Between
1984 and 1991 the number of such cases in New York City has
more than doubled. This tragic and recurrent epidemic is
compounded by crowding, homelessness, the presence of
AIDS, and may well be occurring in other urban centers.

Just recently a genetic mutation that causes resistance in
the tubercle bacillus to the antibiotic drug isoniazid has been
shown to be the deletion of a certain gene. This gene produces
the enzyme catalase which in turn is necessary to activate the
drug's destruction of the bacterial cell; thus absence of the enzyme protects the bacillus against the drug. Genetic altera-
tions such as this one, producing drug resistance, are now appearing in a whole series of diseases including pneumonia,
staphlococcal infections, dysentery, gonorrhea, malaria, and
others. One factor contributing to this development is the
widespread prescribing of antibiotics where they are not spe-
cifically indicated, as, for instance, in viral infections—a practice that usually is promoted by pressure from the patient or
uncertainty on the part of the physician, or both.

The re-emergence of old infectious diseases and the
emergence of new ones, primarily viral, are a cause of real
concern for the public health. Many of these occurrences are
man-made. These human factors include relaxation of vaccination programs, poverty and malnutrition, urbanization,
overpopulation, more rapid mixing of peoples by air trans-

port, and changes in land use and habitat such as the opening up or destruction of tropical forests. All these permit widening contacts between microbes in animal reservoirs and insect or animal vectors (carriers) and, ultimately, human beings.

A few examples must suffice. The building of dams and irrigation projects in Egypt and Mauritania have led to more mosquitoes and these in turn to the spread of Rift Valley fever, and in Panama to the spread of Venezuelan equine encephalitis. In Argentina the conversion of grasslands to maize fields led to a population explosion of field mice carrying the virus of Junin, or Argentine hemorrhagic fever, and thence to many more cases in humans. In the American Southwest a recent increase in rodents has introduced the hantavirus into the Navajo population with a number of fatal cases. In the U. S. Northeast reforestation has caused the deer population to expand with more deer ticks, ticks which carry the spirochete of Lyme disease; as humans live hear the woodlands, there has been a rapid increase in human cases of this potentially crippling disease.

The genetic alteration by mutation of old viruses, or the emergence of new ones, add to the man-made difficulties listed above. The great 1918 pandemic of influenza that killed millions was due to the emergence of a new influenza virus. Since then the "flu" virus, in its primary reservoir in ducks, pigs, and peasants in rural China, has continued to change its genetic character every few years, thus requiring the manufacture of new vaccines repeatedly for the rest of the world. The current prime example of an emergent new pathogenic microorganism is the HIV virus that is causing a world-wide epidemic of lethal autoimmune deficiency disease, or AIDS. This virus appears to have come from the African jungle about 10 years ago when the highway across central Africa from Mombasa to Zaire was opened up, but its exact source and animal reservoir have not yet been identified. There are other viruses undoubtedly present in animal reservoirs, as for example, in the Congo the Marburg and Ebola filoviruses that produce fatal hemorrhagic fever in monkeys; these viruses on a few occasions have emerged and produced fatal disease in humans.

*   *   *

The age of antibiotics, begun so dramatically half a century ago and developed so optimistically over the intervening years, may not be ending but certainly it is changing. The development of microbial resistance to the "miracle drugs" and the emergence of new viral diseases are seeing to that. The time for complacency is over. The wake-up call has been sounded by the Institute of Medicine and by many other scientists. The unending contest in nature between microbes and mankind goes on. And success for mankind, in this contest as in others, depends on eternal vigilance.

Bedford, MA
June, 1993

TRUE BIOLOGICAL WARFARE

Humans should not confuse themselves. This is true biological warfare, in which new drugs designed by humans will become obsolete through bacterial mutations, only to be replaced by human drugs and new bacterial mutations in a seesaw battle. The days of soap and boiling water to fight bacteria are long gone (although soap and boiling water are still useful) and the days of miracle drugs and universal vaccines are going. A long struggle with a premium on basic research to improve our stratagems and applied research to develop new magic bullets is clearly the prognosis for the future. —Daniel E. Kashland, Jr., editorial in *Science*, 15 April 1994.

Brown eggs vs. white

Tub-baths vs. showers

20

From Brown Eggs to the Loch Ness Monster

Minor Notes from Life in the UK

The wit and whimsy embedded in the British character are greeted by his American cousin with delight. This was brought home to me when, in 1972, my English wife and I moved to England to spend the first 13 years of retirement in her beloved homeland. Nowhere are these characteristics more evident than in the British press. In a earlier essay I already have presented examples of this wit and whimsy as manifested in the ongoing torrent of letters to the Editor in *The Times* of London. Now, in browsing through my collection of clippings from that idyllic interlude in the UK, I have come across a few more humorous items that I would like to share with you.

BROWN EGGS VS. WHITE EGGS. This item actually surfaced in the US just before we left for England. *The New*

York Times reprinted excerpts from an article first published in *The New Statesman* by J. B. Priestley, British author and playwright, entitled "The Meaning of Brown Eggs". "Here in England", says Mr. Priestley, "most of us, all ages, prefer brown eggs to white eggs. In America , brown eggs are despised, sold off cheaply, perhaps sometimes thrown away....We English prefer brown eggs because they seem to us to have a more reliable look of rusticity....Americans, well outside ghettos, despise brown eggs just because they do seem closer to nature. White eggs are much better....because their very whiteness suggests hygiene and purity....The weakness of American civilization...is that it is so curiously abstract..."

American readers responded instantly and vigorously. Under the head, "Some Hard-boiled Answers to J. B. Priestley", the *N. Y. Times* published eleven indignant letters defending the brown egg, capped by a piece by E. B. White entitled "Farmer White's Brown Eggs (Cont.)". Mr. White details his long experience producing (courtesy of his chickens) brown eggs that are greatly cherished in New England. He points out that in the Boston produce market brown eggs fetch 3 cents more per dozen than do white eggs. And, he asks, "Why is it, do you suppose" that an Englishman is unhappy until he has explained America?...one seldom meets an American who is all tensed up because he has yet to explain England". So much for Mr. Humpty-dumpty Priestley.

THE ENGLISH BREAKFAST. This subject easily follows since one of its essential ingredients is the egg, whether brown or white. There are those who uphold the puny Continental breakfast and who warn against the calories, cholesterol, and saturated fats of the fried eggs, bacon, and sausages, lying in wait at the center of the standard English breakfast. True, to an American fond of a thin narrow strip of crisp bacon, the English bacon appears more like a large slab of fried ham. But the principle is the same: "Eggs and bacon keep the heart from aching" and are a sound foundation for the day's activities.

In a letter to the London *Times* Sir Dingle Foot writes "in defense of the English breakfast" in which he deprecates an earlier article. The author had praised Prime Minister Heath's customary half-grapefruit and one boiled egg and had boasted of his own single bowl of porridge. "Contrast these matitudinal ascetics", says Sir Dingle, "with some of the great figures in our own literature and history. First of all, Archdeacon Grantly, a description of whose breakfast appears in Trollope's *The Warden*"; Sir Dingle quotes verbatim the long list of foods set out: coffee, toasts, crumpets, breads, eggs, bacon, fish, devilled kidneys, and a huge ham (cold from the previous evening). "Such was the ordinary fare at Plumstead Episcopi". And such should adequately fortify the Archdeacon as he goes forth to do battle with Bishop Proudie and Mr. Slope.

Sir Dingle also notes in *The Pickwick Papers* the astute comment of Mr. Pickwick's lawyer on the way to the hearing of *Bardell v. Pickwick* that "'hungry jurymen always find for the plaintiff'. This may very well be the explanation for the result. The jury had not had an adequate breakfast" As for Lord Palmerston, at age 81, "almost on the last day of his life, he breakfasted off mutton chops and half a glass of old port, exclaiming 'what a good breakfast it is!'

So much for those who decry the English breakfast. Pish! And, what is more, tush!" That should settle it.

TUB-BATH VS. SHOWER. The feature in *The Times* headed "The Times Diary" and by-lined "PHS"—at that time written by reporter Michael Leapman—was a perennial source of delightful trivia from the English scene. For instance, he writes, "My readers are in little doubt about the bathroom problem I posed last week: why Americans make do with short bathtubs?" One reader responded: "Most Amer-

icans prefer to shower rather than to bathe and the bath merely accomodates their feet...bathing is generally equated with
marinating in one's own waste products". An American wrote
in that "the British operate on the soaking principle, the
Americans on the rinsing principle".

This exchange reinforced my own prejudices concerning
bathing in Britain. My English wife considers a hot tub to be
the epitome of luxury; I, as an American habituated to shower
baths, find each tub bath a difficult experience, an awkward
stewing in one's own juice. I look back with sadness on a long
series of these immersions, enforced on me by the mores of
polite society and repeated sojourns in England and Europe.
Some of these baths are more unforgetable than others. There
was, for instance, that bath I took in 1947 in a guest house in
New Milton in Hampshire. I filled the tub too full. When I
climbed in, the water entered the overflow pipe. The overflow
pipe merely ran through the outside wall to deliver its contents just above the kitchen window. The kitchen window
was open and dinner was being prepared just inside. Shouts
of alarm and indignation! Quite evidently nobody had had a
full tub since the beginning of the War. Hard thoughts at dinner: these extravagant Americans, this short-sighted (and
short-piped) English plumbing!

When, forty-five years later, we retired to live in England and bought a house in a village in Herefordshire, nat-
urally one of the first things I did was to install a shower over
the bathtub. The gentle flow of water by gravity from the tank
up under the roof led me to christen this "the mercy shower"
("the quality of mercy is not strained, it droppeth like gentle
rain from heaven...").

Nevertheless, it did the necessary rinsing of the American half of the family.

THE NOMENCLATURE OF WET-WEATHER FOOT-
WARE. The Englishman, fortified with a tub bath and a

hearty breakfast (including brown eggs), must prepare to en-counter the out-of-doors—usually wet. What does he put on his feet if it is not deep enough or muddy enough for welling-tons? (Wellingtons—knee-high heavy rubber boots easily slipped on over stockinged feet—are Britain's greatest con-tribution to this particular need of mankind).

The Times Diary started a long and confusing exchange on this subject by asking "whatever happened, in a week of perpetual rain, to that admirable invention, the galosh? Half the shoe shops in London were scoured for a pair without suc-cess—why?" Leaving aside the answer to that question, the exchange quickly became a sea of confusion over definition and nomenclature. In some parts of the UK, it was claimed that galoshes were called "Jemimas"—whether so named for Beatrix Potter's Jemima Puddleduck, or the duck named for the preexisting footware, was not clear. Others defined Jem-imas as elastic-sided leather boots and not as galoshes ("galoshes", apparently, are the Btitish name for what Amer-icans call "rubber overshoes" or "rubbers".) "Galoshes" in the US refer to short flexible boots that can be zipped on over reg-ular shoes, and sometimes are also called "arctics"—which in-formation I passed on to "The Diary". I also pointed out that, whatever "Jemimas" were in the UK, in the US they were more likely to be thought of as something good to eat, name-ly, Aunt Jemima's pancakes.

So much for misunderstandings in nomenclature be-tween the two cultures.

CRICKET VS. BASEBALL. Another cross-cultural quag-mire lies in the field of sports. During my many years of vis-iting and living in Britain I have endeavored, rather in-effectually, to understand the intricacies of the game of cricket. Our village butcher, Peter, a stalwart member of the village cricket team, kept trying to develop my understanding of the sport. Each time a Test match was held somewhere in the British Commonwealth, Peter would try to elucidate for me the happenings and nuances of the game then being played and televised. Each year during the baseball World Series in the US I would try to explain to Peter what was happening in that game over there. I am afraid that success in these explanatory sessions was not very complete. Perhaps it was more like trying to explain to my English neighbors, at the time, the political complexities of Watergate. Well, so be it. Each nation seems addicted to, if not satisfied with, its own sports as well as with its own politics.

An American's idea of cricket

An Englishman's idea of baseball

PETS—TANGIBLE AND INTANGIBLE. No people are more devoted to the enjoyment, care, and defense of their pets than the British . But here I do not refer to the lovers of cats and dogs who seem to be in unending and vehement conflict with each other and with the other's pets. Rather, I am intrigued with certain intangible—indeed mythical—pets that seem to be ongoing national obsessions . Here are two.

The first is *Winnie-the-Pooh*, the endearing Pooh, "the Bear of Very Little Brain", a character created by A. A. Milne in the stories for his son, Christopher Robin. Pooh and his companions, Piglet, Eeyore, Rabbit, and all the others, inhabiting the "Enchanted Wood" (in Sussex), for more than half a century have delighted children the world over. Indeed, the Pooh books have been translated into a great many other languages, including Latin where Pooh appears as "Edwardus Ursis" in *Winnie-ille-Pu*.

All this was brought to mind by a charming piece in *The Times* by John Rae, headmaster of Westminster School (which school Pooh's creator, A. A. Milne, once attended). "Pooh, the most English teddy bear", speculated Mr. Rae, had a wide appeal in cultures that are Christian, affluent, and with a low infant mortality, where childhood is considered a separate age of innocence. Pooh's prolonged and widespread popularity he attributed to the expertise of Milne's writing and the brilliant simplicity of Ernest Shepard's illustrations; together they produced an ideal world "where springs did not fail" and where for Pooh there was always honey for tea.

The ensuing correspondence in *The Times* explores the question of the original bear on which Pooh was modelled. There was Winnie, the brown bear in the London Zoo (a former mascot of the Canadian Army during World War I); Milne's young son was known to have visited this bear, at which time he is reputed to have exclaimed "Oh, pooh!". More probably, the teddy bear named "Growler" and belonging to Shepard's son, Graham, was the model used by Shepard for his drawings of Pooh.

Pooh Bear, with honey pot and friends

—After E. H. Shepard

The winning character of Pooh continues to intrigue his admirers who exist far beyond the British Isles. An American magazine revealed that an Australian physician, Dr. J. E. Gault, diagnosed Pooh as suffering from spontaneous functional hypoglycemia. This diagnosis was based on Pooh's "coming all over funny" at 11 o'clock in the morning and having to hurry home to empty a pot of honey.

Despite such an entertaining medical handicap, Pooh has even been claimed to personify Taoism, as presented in a recent little volume, *The Tao of Pooh*, (written, I might say, not by a Chinese but by a Westerner).

Pooh, despite all this, is still primarily a favorite, though intangible, English pet, with his feet and his honey pots firmly planted in Britain.

A second legendary "pet" obsessing the British mind—a "pet" even more intangible than Pooh—is Nessie, the Loch Ness Monster. Nessie has a somewhat longer history than

Pooh; the first sightings of this large mysterious creature in the waters of that loch in the Highlands of Scotland, are said to go back to 565 A.D. when it was confronted by no less a witness than St, Columba. Gaelic legend had it that the "water horse" could only be lured to land by 24 Scottish virgins (perhaps thus explaining the creature's elusiveness). However, in modern times there have been a multitude of sightings.

The first contacts (if such a term can be used in reference to so intangible an object) that the author of this essay had with Nessie go back many decades. The first reseach fellow to come from Britain to my laboratory in Philadelphia, forty years ago, once assured me that, when he was a boy growing up in Inverness at the foot of Loch Ness, he himself had seen Nessie. Ten years later, on a family visit to Scotland including Loch Ness, our 13 year old son Joe was convinced that the wind streak on the Loch was due to Nessie progressing just below the surface. I, of course, have no reason to disbelieve the belief of either of these observers as to what they saw (or in Joe's case, in what he thought he saw). These "contacts" clearly typify the whole Loch Ness Monster saga.

When we went to live in England during the 1970s and 1980s, the obsession of the British with their Highland "pet" boiled up yet again in the British press, especially in *The Times*. In 1976 a report appeared about the aeronautical engineer, Tim Dinsdale, who had retired 15 years before to live on a small boat on the Loch in order to look for the Monster. He had seen it three times and was convinced that it is a large marine animal, about 40 feet long, possibly similar to the long-extinct Jurassian plesiosaur. Hundreds of sightings of multiple humps, a long neck with a large head, and long wakes, have been reported—especially since a new road brought more tourists alongside the Loch. Underwater photographs and sonar scans were undertaken in the murky waters by the Boston Academy of Applied Science and the results (in-

cluding pictures of flippers) were presented to a symposium
(eschewed by the scientific Establishment) held in the House
of Commons.

Subsequent epistolary comments ranged from "The
credulous in pursuit of the fabulous" and "Man measures galaxies and brings back chunks of the moon by hand but cannot
determine whether an object a few fathoms below the surface
is an aquatic creature or a bit of old Viking rubbish" to longer
letters from less doubting, though still skeptical, more distinguished correspondents. Sir Peter Scott, naturalist, discussed the pros and cons and explained why no floating
corpses of the creatures had appeared; later in an article in *Nature* he even gave the creature a formal scientific name: *Nes-
siterus rhomboteryx*. Sir Robert McEwen commented that, con-
sidering the multitude of photographs, films, radar scans, and
ordinary sightings (over 3000 since 1933), "it is not the observer who is at fault, it is that attitude of mind of the people who
think they know better". Philip Howard, columnist at *The
Times,,* wrote of one scientist who believed in a surviving family of plesiosaurs from late Jurassic seas (he lost his job in the
British Museum).

"Now he shows up . . .
Where was he in the tourist season?"

—Courtesy of cartoonist
Kailes (?) source unknown

Such a view of "drop-outs from the evolutionary rat race" received short shrift from the zoological Establishment which explained all observations as "deliberate hoaxes by interested hotel-keepers, errors by the stupid, delusions by the nutty, or floating logs, otters, swimming deer, cormorants magnified by mist, or other infinite variations of human silliness or suggestibility". Eight years later, in 1984, Howard reported the "latest garbage about the monster": a plan for "a gigantic mousetrap, baited with old fish, to trap Nessie". Clearly, the British obsession predates the current American dinosaurian frenzy over Hollywood's "Jurassic Park"!

The very latest (July 1993) science news item from Loch Ness is NOT of an actual body, alive or dead, weighed and measured. Rather, it is of the discovery on the Loch's bottom of a unique new nematode—a worm a few millimeters long. Not quite our Nessie. But just wait, Nessie must be there awaiting the day of tangible revelation yet to come—perhaps.

* * *

Oh, to be in England now that all these, too, are there: hearty English breakfasts with BROWN eggs and bacon, at least a few more shower-baths recently installed, wellington boots and galoshes—no matter what they are called, cricket with all its leisurely activity and traditional ritual, and pets of the less-tangible variety—Pooh Bear humming in the minds of children and (north of the Border) Nessie lurking in the depths of Loch Ness!

September, 1993

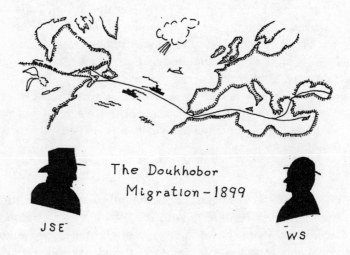

The Doukhobor
Migration – 1899

JSE

WS

Joseph S. Elkinton, A Quaker receiver, and
Wilson Sturge, A Quaker sender of
the Doukhobors from Russia to Canada

21

Quakers and the Russian Bear

A few years after my English wife, Teresa, and I were married more than fifty years ago, we discovered a previously unsuspected link between our respective English and American families. In 1899, nearly half a century before our marriage, two of our Quaker forbears, her grandfather and my great-grandfather, had manned the two ends of a trans-Atlantic lifeline for the emigration of more than seven thousand religious refugees from Russia to Canada. These were the Doukhobors, a dissenting and pacifist Christian sect who were fleeing the savage persecution of Russia's Czarist Government.

Before we come to the story of the Doukhobors and the involvement of our two families in that story, it is worth commenting on the long history over the preceding two centuries of Quaker contacts with the rulers of Russia, contacts made for the promotion of peace and for humanitarian relief.

Encounters in the 18th and Early 19th Centuries

These contacts began with the young Czar, Peter the Great (1672-1725), the founder of St. Petersburg, who came incognito to England in 1698 to learn how to build ships. While at the Deptford shipyard he attended a nearby Quaker meeting for worship; apparently he was greatly impressed and was encouraged in his efforts to improve the lot of his people. The next contact was later in the 18th Century when, in 1768, Empress Catherine II, the Great (1729-1796), wrote to the eminent Quaker physician in London, Dr. John Fothergill, asking him to come to St. Petersburg to inoculate herself and her son against smallpox. Dr. Fothergill, (who happens to be a collateral ancestor of my wife), could not go but sent in his stead another Quaker physician, Dr. Thomas Dimsdale, who successfully performed the inoculations. (The elaborate plans that had been prepared for Dr. Dimsdale's escape should the outcome prove otherwise—that is, a royal fatality—were not needed). Consequently the Empress conferred on Dr. Dimsdale the title of Baron, which title later proved to be somewhat detrimental to the Doctor's expected Quaker humility.

In 1815, while Czar Alexander I (1777-1825) was in London for diplomatic negotiations, English Quakers addressed him on the issue of anti-slavery. The Czar, a very sensitive and religious man, made friends with two Quaker leaders, William Allen and Stephen Grellet, and asked to attend a Quaker Meeting for worship. With his retinue in full uniform, he did so and was greatly impressed. After his return to St. Petersburg, the Emperor wrote to William Allen asking if there were a Quaker agriculturist who would come to St. Petersburg to drain and then cultivate the intractable marshes surrounding the city. Daniel Wheeler, a Quaker from Sheffield, felt the call to respond and, in 1817, went to St. Petersburg, made an agreement with the Czar, and returned the next year with his wife and six children plus a number of assistants and their families. The Wheeler party stayed for 15 years and were completely successful in draining the marshes and in establishing model farms on the Crown lands outside the city. Sadly, Daniel Wheeler's wife and one daughter died of cholera and were buried in a special little graveyard deeded by the Russian Government to the Society of Friends; it is a memorial to Quaker outreach that still is visited today.

"Deputation to the Czar 1854", Panel No. 34 in the Quaker Tapestry, Kendal England. The panel was designed by Deborah Mason and the Tapestry group and was worked by Griselda Mary Mason.

Reproduced by permission of the Quaker Tapestry Scheme

The next Quaker approach to the Russian Bear was in 1854. Britain and France were threatening Russia over the protection of Christians in Turkey's Ottoman Empire. Joseph Sturge of Birmingham, merchant, philanthropist, abolitionist, (and my wife's great-great uncle), believed that a religious address to Czar Nicholas I might help to avert war. The Society of Friends in London agreed and sent Joseph Sturge and two other Friends, Robert Charleton and Henry Pease, on a hasty trip to St. Petersburg. In the dead of winter (January-February) this was no mean feat as the railway ended in Konisberg in Prussia and the remaining 650 miles to St. Petersburg had to be traversed first by horse-drawn carriage and then by sledge. Despite several overturnings into deep snowdrifts, they arrived safely; the whole trip from London had taken 15 days.

After some delay the Quaker deputation was graciously received by the Czar. Joseph Sturge read the address urging the Czar to follow Christ's path of peace and to resolve the conflict by negotiation; the Czar responded sympathetically but stated that the outcome was up to the opposing Powers. By the time the deputation got back to London 9 days later, the shrill tones of the British press and Parliament had made the Crimean War inevitable. The Quakers had not succeeded in averting war but they had made the great effort that their consciences had called for.

Quakers and the Doukhobors in the Late 19th and 20th Centuries

In Russia

Now we come to the story of the Doukhobors and of the parts played in that story by the Society of Friends (Quakers) including members of our own two families. The Doukhobors, or "Spirit-Wrestlers", were one of a series of dissenting religious sects in Russia during the 18th Century that arose against the forms of the Russian Orthodox Church. They mostly were peasants who believed in a primitive Christianity without priests, held land in common, and eschewed violence. As they were against military conscription, they brought down the wrath of the Government of Czar Nicholas I and many were banished to Trans-Caucasian Georgia. During the last few decades of the 19th Century Count Leo Tolstoy, himself a radical dissenter from the Orthodox Church, became interested in the Doukhobors and gave them his support. So likewise did the Quakers in England and America who also were sympathetic with their beliefs and their pacifism.

In 1892-93 two British Quakers, Joseph James Neave and John Bellows, made a prolonged journey to Russia to visit some of these dissenters including the Doukhobors. A fascinating account of this journey is set forth in the volume *John Bellows: Letters and Memoir.* John Bellows was a widely travelled Quaker printer, lexicographer, and antiquarian from Gloucester, (and, incidentally, was a relative of my wife as well as a friend of my own grandparents). In Moscow Neave and Bellows visited Count Tolstoy and he and John Bellows developed a warm friendship. Tolstoy advised the two Quakers to visit the Doukhobors in the Trans-Caucasus. This they did, crossing the high mountain passes by horse-drawn carriage. In Tiflis and throughout Georgia they found the Doukhobors, who earlier had been banished to this Trans-Caucasian area, to be farming quite successfully among a great ethnic mixture of Georgians, Armenians, Turks, and Persians (a mixture that 100 years later led to the present violent ethnic civil warfare). While in Georgia John Bellows went to Poti on the Black Sea to visit his Quaker friend, Wilson Sturge, who at that time was British Vice-Consul in that port. Wilson Sturge it was who later organized part of the Doukhobor emigration from Cyprus to Canada. Bellows and Neave, after another visit to Tolstoy, returned to Britain, thus ending their half-year journey. Three years later, in 1896, the Doukhobors rebelled against the military conscription that recently had been extended to the Trans-Caucasian area. On the same night in several districts of Georgia, to show their renunciation of violence, they held ceremonial burnings of all their weapons. The Czarist Government immediately sent in Cossack troops who beat, jailed, or killed many of the men and drove their families from their homes. At this point, the Doukhobors, many thousands in number, decided that emigration from Russia was their only hope. They turned for help to their religious sympathizers, Count Tolstoy and his supporters in Russia and the Quakers in Britain and America. The island of Cyprus and the Dominion of Canada both indicated a willingness to receive them. In March 1898, through intercession by the Dowager Empress with her son the Czar, the Russian Government gave the Doukhobors permission to leave.

There is an interesting little side-light to the efforts of Tolstoy and the Quakers to raise money for this major Doukhobor relief project. Tolstoy dug up the unpublished manuscript of what proved to be his last novel, "Resurrection", had it published, and sent the immediate royalties of 150 pounds to his friend, John Bellows, then chairman of the Quaker Committee on Doukhobors in London . When John Bellows and his wife read the novel with its explicit descriptions of the life and rehabilitation of a prostitute, they were horrified and Bellows sent the money back. Tolstoy's response to John Bellows was understanding and apologetic, and was revealing of himself as a novelist. In part, he wrote: "I hope that the reader...will find out what the author likes or dislikes, and will be influenced by the sentiments of the author, and I can say that when I wrote the book I abhorred with all my heart the lust, and to express this abhorrence was one of the chief aims of the book".

The Emigration

In September 1898 a portion of the desperate Doukhobors, 1100 in number, sailed from Bartoum on the Black Sea
to Cyprus where some 1500 acres of farmland had been of-
fered them. But here there were only tents to shelter them, the
land was damp and malarial, and the immigrants were ill-
equipped to farm it successfully. To help them the Quaker
Committee in London sent out Wilson Sturge (my wife's
grandfather), a Quaker businessman from Birmingham who
had been British Vice-Consul in Poti in the Caucasus for six
years and had become well-acquainted with the Doukhobors.
When he got to Cyprus he found "a prospect little short of ap-
palling". He and a few younger assistants, including William
Bellows (son of John), did the best they could with a dis-
astrous situation and recommended that these Doukhobors in
Cyprus be sent to Canada to join the rest who were being
shipped there directly from Russia.

This was done later in the next year, 1899. After em-
barking these difficult and hapless refugees on one of the two
steamships chartered by the Quakers in London for the purpose of transporting all the Doukhobors to Canada, Wilson
Sturge stayed behind to wind up their affairs in Cyprus and
then sailed for England. Sadly, on the voyage home his health
failed, he died, and was buried on Malta. He was in his 65th
year and had been greatly beloved by his Russian charges in
Cyprus who called him "Good Grandfather".

Meanwhile, in January 1899, the first contingent of
Doukhobors, some 2000 in number, who had embarked in Ba-
toum on the steamship *Lake Huron*, arrived in Halifax, Nova
Scotia. Here they were met by Prince Hillkoff, an exiled dis-
sident Russian aristocrat who had assisted in the negotiations
with the Canadian authorities, and by two American Quakers.
One of these was Job Gidley from Massachusetts and the oth-

er was Joseph S. Elkinton of Philadelphia. The latter was a
leading minister in the Orthodox branch of the Society of
Friends as well as a manufacturer, an active worker for the
rights of native American Indians and negro ex-slaves, and, as
it happens, my great-grandfather. In his diary he tells of going
down on the tugboat with the quarantine officials to meet the
ship:

> "As we approached and came up opposite the windward
> side, it was a wonderful sight: the children in the front and the
> length of the ship made an imposing sight. Most of them had
> on sheepskin coats with the wool inside, the girls in front of
> the women and the boys in front of the men; and all joined in a
> subdued but melodious and distinct tone in chanting words
> which Prince Hillkoff afterward translated for me. It was a
> very affecting scene, and the spirit of thanksgiving and prayer
> covered my mind. Job Gidley broke forth with the salutation in
> a clear strong voice, 'Welcome Doukhobors'...[On board], with
> a continued feeling of the spirit of prayer, I gave expression on
> bended knee to my exercise...The translation of their [the
> Doukhobors'] offering in chorus, given me by Prince Hillkoff,
> is as follows: 'Know all men. God is with us. He has carried us
> through. We uplift our voice and sing his praise. They that
> planned our ruin did not succeed...' I felt that if ever I heard
> the voice of thanksgiving and melody from human lips, I did
> on that notable occasion".

After this "notable occasion" of welcome, the ship was
cleared by the quarantine officials and the two Quakers pro-
ceeded on board with the immigrants to the port of St. John,
New Brunswick. Here the Doukhobors were entrained for
Winnipeg and the areas on the plains of of the Canadian
Northwest Territory that had been promised them for settle-
ment. On this passage to St. John, Grandfather reported that
he was approached by an old man "who said that I reminded
him of the visit of two Friends in Russia in the year 1818. I

told him that they were Stephen Grellett and Daniel Wheeler; I had seen them both. 'I saw them, I saw them', he said, 'and now I see you as another messenger from the Lord'". After seeing the immigrants off on the trains, Great-grandfather and his Quaker companion returned to Halifax to await the second shipload of Doukhobors.

This ship, the *Lake Superior*, arrived ten days after the *Lake Huron*, but because of a case of smallpox on board was held in quarantine; Great-grandfather returned to Philadelphia. In mid-February the ship was cleared and, despite a blizzard that for two days blocked the tracks between Philadelphia and New York, Great-grandfather, with Job Gidley, returned to Halifax. There they greeted this second contingent of Doukhobors, this time accompanied by Count Tolstoy's son, Sergius, and saw them on board the Canadian Pacific trains bound for Winnipeg. Great-grandfather went with them as far as Ottawa where he interviewed Canadian officials on their behalf.

Later in the spring and summer two more shiploads of Doukhobors arrived in Canada. In May the *Lake Superior* reached Quebec carrying the 1030 immigrants that Wilson Sturge had sent off from Cyprus. They were accompanied by his young associate, William Bellows. Joseph S. Elkinton went up to meet them and then travelled with them as far as Ottawa on their way west, before returning home . In June he again travelled to Quebec to meet the fourth and last contingent on the *Lake Huron*. As there was a case of smallpox on board, the ship was quarantined for three weeks. During this time Great-grandfather journeyed out to Manitoba to visit, inspect, and hold religious services among the earlier immigrants in the many primitive settlements that they had set up in the province. In July, when the quarantine of the ship had been lifted, he returned to Quebec to greet the Doukhobors on board and again to accompany them as far as Ottawa on their way west to join the others in their new settlements.

Thus, in the first six months of 1899, more than seven thousand of these persecuted Doukhobors—7,363 to be exact— had been brought from Russia to new homes in the Canadian West. This was said to be the largest single group of immigrants ever to have come to North America.

In Canada

The subsequent history during the 20th Century of the Doukhobors in Canada can only be summarized briefly here. They were a sturdy, colorful, and industrious people who arrived in Canada utterly destitute of material wealth. Put down on the bare prairies with severe winter weather ahead and with almost no tools, building materials, or money, they had initially just the rough shelters and supplies of food provided by the Canadian Government and the Society of Friends. Nevertheless they set about vigorously establishing a wide network of villages scattered across the prairies of Manitoba and Saskatchewan. Most of the work was done by the women who outnumbered the men three to one. Many of the husbands had been killed or jailed in Russia and most of those who did reach Canada had to hire themselves out as laborers on other farms or on the railways to earn a little cash; hence they were away for weeks or months. The women perforce rose to the occasion by dragging logs, making mortar out of clay for plastering, building the sod-roofed log houses, and carrying on their shoulders sacks of flour from many miles away. As many of the villages had only one yoke of oxen or one pair of horses, the women pulled the ploughs to break the prairie and sowed the fields that they created. They were a doughty people!

But the Doukhobors also were a strong-willed and extremely obstinate people who resisted any changes to their religious beliefs and to their customs of holding property in common, of refusing military service, and of giving only oral education to their children. Initially these customs led to stubborn conflicts with the Canadian authorities over registration of births, marriages, and deaths, and especially over education of their children in the public schools. The degree and pace of resolution of these conflicts varied among different Doukhobor groups. The more progressive ones who decided to register their lands individually became known as "Independents"; they were assimilated more rapidly into Canadian life. Many, however, continued to live and farm communally and became known as "Community Doukhobors"; they were slower to adapt.

In 1903 the Doukhobors' young ex-leader, Peter Verigin, who had been in jail in Siberia during the emigration, was released and came out to Canada. Insisting on strict adherence to traditional customs, he ably organized and improved the farming practices of the Community Doukhobors. In 1912 he decided to move several thousand of them from Saskatchewan to southern British Columbia where they purchased 15,000 acres in the Kootenay valley. Here, still living in communes, they became very successful fruit farmers.

Nevertheless, there remained among them a small but very fanatical minority, calling themselves the "Sons of Freedom", who continued to resist totally the authorities in these settlements. These zealots repeatedly burned down the schools built for their children and demonstrated by parading naked through the streets, thereby scandalizing their Canadian neighbors. In 1924 Verigin mysteriously was killed by a bomb on his train. In 1950 several hundred members of this small minority were jailed and their children placed in boarding schools. But arson still plagued the community as late as 1983 when several of their community centers were burned

Doukhobors in Canada - Early Days

Scenes from the book (1903) by Joseph Elkinton
Photographs by himself and William Bellows.

Doukhobor costumes showing prayer sash and marriage scarf. The man is Joseph Elkinton wearing garments given as a gift.

"Grandmother Verigin, mother of the Doukhobor leader in prison in Siberia, and Patriarch Ivan Mahortov, the "old man" who remembered seeing the Quaker visitors to Russia in 1818.

Doukhobor girls in front of sod-roofed log houses, chanting in welcome to visitors.

Doukhobor women drawing plough.
There is a shortage of horses and oxen; The men are away either in prison in Siberia or working on the Canadian railroads to earn some cash. So the women have volunteered.

down. Thus these intransigent fanatics, a mere one percent of all the Doukhobors in Canada, persisted as a thorn in the sides of the Government and the Quakers and severely damaged the reputation of all the rest of the Doukhobors who had become responsible Canadian citizens.

During this 20th Century somewhat tumultuous assimilation of these Russian Doukhobors into the New World, Quakers in Britain, Canada, and the United States, strove to assist them. This they did by providing supplies of food and seeds for planting, by promoting proper education for the children, by religious visiting, and by interceding with frustrated Canadian authorities. Quaker teachers were provided: from Britain, Helen Morland and Hannah Bellows, from Canada, Eliza Varney and Nellie Baker; and from Ireland, a nurse, Sara Boyle.

In this ongoing effort four generations of my own Elkinton family have been much involved. My great-grandfather, Joseph S. Elkinton, between 1899 and 1903, at the age of 70 to 73 years, made in all eight visits to greet and settle these Doukhobors in their new Canadian home. As his son wrote about his father: "To go from village to village and from house to house, travelling hundreds of miles over the open prairie in order to comfort those to whom he could not speak in their native language, extending sympathy and encouragement as well as distributing food and clothing, is very typical of his lifework. The Canadian officials valued his services enough to send for him more than once when they could not manage these difficult immigrants."

This son, my grandfather, Joseph Elkinton, not only assisted his father before the latter's death in 1905 but carried on the work to within two years of his own death in 1920. During this time he visited and photographed the Doukhobors frequently and wrote a book about their history and emigration. In his book, published in 1903, he expressed his concern about the need for education of these newly-arrived immigrants, a concern that he repeatedly conveyed to them in person. He wrote:

> "To educate and develop into loyal citizens of a free State a people who for a century have suffered persecution and even martyrdom for conscience' sake at the hands of their rulers, requires the utmost tact and wisdom. The disinclination that they all felt to accepting such instruction from the Government schools was the natural result of the cruel treatment they had previously received in Russia...
>
> Yet, ...their enlightenment is not a hopeless undertaking by any means. The high moral standard they maintain, and their thrift, bear ample evidence of a right development of mind in many respects. But their inability to see that their spiritual interests do not necessarily conflict with such sane institutions as the homestead and registration laws and the public school system, reveals a crudeness of mind which cannot be overcome at once".

But as indicated above, eventually, for the most part, these conflicts were resolved.

In 1902 Grandfather's immediate contribution to this resolution was to bring a family with five children down to live for the winter in his own home outside Philadelphia so that the children could go to the local Friends' School and learn some English. This was not easy for his wife, Grandmother Sarah Elkinton, but it paid off; the youngest boy, Peter Makaroff, returned to become the first Doukhobor to gain a college degree, and to graduate from the University's Law School in Saskatchewan.

During subsequent years, my father, Passmore Elkinton, as well as his brother Howard, made many visits to the Doukhobors. Indeed, in 1921 he took his 11-year old son, the author of this essay, on a business trip to the West Coast and, returning across Canada, we stayed with Peter Makaroff in Saskatoon; a few years later Father took my younger brother on a similar visit. In my generation, the chief family contacts with the Doukhobors have been made by my cousin Peter (son of Howard) and by my brother, David Elkinton. He last visited many of them in 1983 and has been involved with the Doukhobor historian, Koozma Tarasoff, in recording the history of these Russian immigrants over the 20th Century.

*   *   *

Thus ends my story of Quaker encounters with "the Russian Bear", encounters involving my wife's kith and kin in England and my own family in America. Of course there have been many other Quakers who have encountered the Russians—especially during the terrible famines in the early 1920s shortly after the Revolution. But that is another story. And now, in the present chaotic state of the Russian Bear after the breakup of the Soviet Union, who knows what lies ahead for Quakers, and indeed for the whole world? Whatever may be the situation, let us hope that again there will be compassion, understanding, and strength and wisdom to help our fellow human beings of this enormous land in their times of need.

March, 1994

BELLOWS ON TOLSTOY*

Letter: John Bellows to Joseph Elkinton, Philadelphia.

GLOUCESTER, 8 January, 1900

"As Count Tolstoi has all along been so deeply interested in this migration of the Doukhobortsi, and feels so earnestly for the Siberian exiles, we arranged to go over to Moscow and see him.

"We dined and spent the evening with Count Tolstoi and his family, and with one or two of their friends. . . Our welcome was warm by every one of the family, who, like all those who saw Joseph James Neave and myself seven years ago, enquired very lovingly after him, and were not a little interested to hear of his being in America now.

"I have been unable to approve of some of Tolstoi's views, or of things he has written; and yet in sitting down by his side I felt the same deep and precious unity of spirit with him which I experienced at our last visit. Grasping both my hands, he said with emotion, 'I have *great* love for you'; and he afterwards adverted to that broadness of mind which enables us to recognise the love of the truth in those who may not be of the same mould of thought as ourselves. Count Tolstoi was earnest that we should leave no possible stone unturned on this errand."

—John Bellows: *Letters and Memoir*, 1904

* In 1899 John Bellows had returned to Russia with a Quaker petition for the release of some 110 Doukhobor exiles in Siberia so that they might join their brethren in Canada. The errand was not successful.

22

Books and the World Inside One's Head

"Books, old familiar books, my long-loved books—how can I bear to part with them?" This must be the central thought of any aging lover of books as he or she sits looking at the shelves of his or her personal library and ponders the inexorable contractions of bookshelf space that lie ahead. Which of these cherished volumes, accumulated over a lifetime, must be discarded and which can be kept for yet a little longer? Which books to keep for the twilight years when the inner need for support by the familiar surely will be greater than ever? What is the role of books in one's life? Hence these reflections.

Books, as much as personal experience, are the building blocks of the mental world in which we live. Books furnish and nourish the ever-developing mind that each of us carries around in his head. Inside that head, the seat of all these mental activities, is the human brain containing nearly a trillion component cells; with its neuronal networks and chemical neurotransmitters the human brain is the most complicated organized biological entity yet to have evolved on this planet. But we are not concerned here with the age-old dilemma of how the physical brain relates to the process going on within it, the process that we call the mind and that is manifested by consciousness and memory. Rather let me consider, from my own experience, the enrichment of that process by the reading of books over a lifetime.

To conjure up the titles of all the books that, over more than eighty years, have contributed to my own mental world is far beyond the scope of this essay. I can only illustrate the process by indicating some of the fields of reading and some of the long-cherished books involved. Perhaps such a nostalgic exercise will help me choose which volumes to select for my anticipated restricted bedside. Undoubtedly there will be too many to physically take with me, in which case I will have to depend on my memory (if I have any left).

*   *   *

BOOKS OF CHILDHOOD. Books from the start of one's read-to and reading life usually consist of stories or fantasies, or both, and add greatly to childhood's developing mental picture of the world. Animals imbued with human personalities are remembered with great fondness: Mole and Ratty and their friends in Kenneth Grahame's *The Wind in the Willows*, Brer Rabbit and Brer Fox in *Uncle Remus* by Joel Chandler Harris, the animal characters in Rudyard Kipling's *Jungle Books* and *Just So Stories*, and the immortal Peter Rabbit, Mrs Tiggywinkle, and all the others created by Beatrix Potter. Add to these, for the more recent generations of our children and grandchildren, Pooh Bear, Piglet, Eeyore, and friends in A. A. Milne's *Winnie the Pooh* books, and Wilbur the pig and Charlotte the spider in E. B. White's jewel, *Charlotte's Web*.

Many human characters, real and fictional, contributed to my expanding mental world. These included King Arthur and his knights, Robin Hood, Jim Hawkins and Long John Silver in Stevenson's *Treasure Island,* and longbowman Aylward and fellow soldiers and knights in Conan Doyle's *The White Company*—these two latter volumes illustrated by the glorious paintings of N. C. Wyeth. And there was the delightful little book, acquired by my mother in 1905, *Darby O'Gill and the Good People* by Hermione Templeton (who was she?) recounting hilarious adventures in the land of Irish fantasy.

STORIES OF THE SEA. *Two Years Before the Mast* by Richard Dana introduced me to the wide world of the sea. Fictional stories of life at sea are myriad. A few old favorites are *Lord Jim* (Conrad), *Moby Dick* (Melville—my copy is illustrated by the marvelous black and white cuts of Rockwell Kent), *The Bounty Trilogy* (Nordoff and Hall), and C. S. Foster's *Horatio Hornblower* series. The two epic poems of *Dauber* by Masefield and *M'Andrew's Hymn* by Kipling vividly evoke life on the great square-rigged clipper ships and in the engineer's world of the old tramp steamers; here are brought to the mind's eye the poignant extremes of strength and weakness of the human spirit. For an overall and in-depth description of the oceans of the globe few books can surpass Rachel Carson's *The Sea Around Us.*

EXPLORATION, MOUNTAINEERING, TRAVEL. No genre of books is more likely to expand the horizons of the young mind. Classic stories are told of Antarctic exploration: of Captain Robert Scott's heroic, flawed, and fatal dash to the South Pole in *Scott's Last Expedition,* in *Edward Wilson of the Antarctic* of Dr. Wilson's scientific and artistic contributions to that expedition, of Ernest Shackleton's account in *South* of his 600 mile open boat voyage to South Georgia to rescue his crew after their ship had been crushed by the pack ice, of Douglas Mawson, sole survivor of the party seeking the South

Magnetic Pole in *Mawson's Will: the Greatest Survival Story Ever Written* (Bickel). As for the Arctic, Vilhjalmur Stefansson's *The Friendly Arctic* told how he pioneered living by hunting on the ice like the Eskimos, and the more recently published *Arctic Grail* (Berton) tells the fascinating stories of the quests for the Northwest Passage and the North Pole between 1818 and 1909, including the search for, and the strange fate of, the Franklin Expedition.

The annals of mountaineering the world over attest again and again to the extremes of human skill, courage, and endurance. There is Edward Whymper's *Scrambles in the Alps* with his account of the first ascent of the Matterhorn and the tragic deaths of four members of his party of seven (I found my second-hand copy in Leary's Bookstore in Philadelphia more than 60 years ago). Great first ascents in the Himalayas—with both triumph and tragedy—are told in *The Conquest of Everest* (Hunt), *Nanga Parbat* (Herrtigkoffer), *Annapurna* (Herzog), *Everest the Hard Way: the First Ascent of the Southwest Face* (Bonington).

Books narrating travels are almost as numerous as there are places on the globe to travel to. I will begin with Swedish Sven Hedin exploring Central Asia early in the last century, follow with *Tent Life in Siberia* in which George Kennan writes of his attempt, later in that century, to survey a telegraph line across the volcanic peninsula of Kamchatka, and end with *The Yangtse Valley and Beyond* in which that indomitable Englishwoman Isabella Bird recounts her 1896-97 trip, at the age of 65, across China to the heights of Tibet—mainly by sedan chair.

THE AMERICAN WEST. My mental pictures of the Far West surely began with the two volumes of prints of George Catlin's paintings of Indian life on the northern Great Plains in the early 19th Century—entrancing volumes discovered by me as a small boy on the book-shelves of a great-aunt. The mental pictures expanded as I grew older, devouring such books as *Life On the Mississippi* and *Roughing It* (Mark Twain), *Year of Decision—1846* (DeVoto), *The Virginian* (Wister), *Exploration of the Colorado River* (Powell), *Death Comes to the Archbishop* (Cather), *Angle of Repose* (Stegner), and *Basin and Range* in which John McPhee explains the geologic dynamics of the formation of the Continent and global plate tectonics.

THE WORLD OF NATURE. Many books bring the great outdoors into our homes and heads. Nature in New England lives in *Walden* by Henry David Thoreau as well as in *The Outermost House* and *Northern Farm* by Henry Beston; nature in the West lives in *The Wilderness World of John Muir* (ed. Teale)—who can forget John Muir's description of his ecstasy as, high in a great Douglas Spruce in a forest on the Sierra Nevada, he rode out a roaring gale off the Pacific? And nature across the whole Continent is told in *Wild America* by Roger Tory Peterson and James Fisher. There are many more.

FICTION, POETRY, DRAMA. Novels, indeed, are too many to be listed; novelists of the 19th Century seem to predominate. Dickens (especially with the *Pickwick Papers*), Eliot, Thackeray, Hardy, Tolstoy, James, Trollope—particularly Trollope whose Barchester and Parliamentary novels my wife and I have read aloud at bedtime over and over for more than fifty years. Mysteries that have entertained include those of Conan Doyle (*Sherlock Holmes*), Dorothy Sayres, and Agatha Christie. Drama starts with Shakespeare and goes on with Shaw. Poetry is represented in Masefield, Kipling, Frost, and a series of anthologies: *Oxford Book of English Verse, Modern Poetry* (Untermeyer), *The Gipsy Trail* (Goldmark and Hopkins), and that epic masterpiece by Robert Bridges, *The Testament of Beauty.*

BIOGRAPHIES AND AUTOBIOGRAPHIES. These are rich sources for building our mental pictures of our fellow humans, and how they have reacted to their worlds. Medical biographies, especially, sit on my shelves, such as those of *Dr. John Fothergill* (Fox, Booth and Corner), *Sir William Osler* (Cushing), and *As I Remember Him,* the autobiography of Hans Zinsser who was one of the great and most dynamic of my medical teachers. The life and thought of Justice Oliver Wendell Holmes is told in *Yankee From Olympus* by Catherine Drinker Bowen and her little book *Adventures of a Biographer* delightfully explores the art of such writing. Diaries, of course, are fascinating autobiographical sources; I will mention only one, *Kilvert's Diary,* which reveals a young curate's inner life and its outer milieu of early Victorian country life on the borders of Wales.

PHYSIOLOGY AND MEDICINE. By now most of the books of my former professional life have left my shelves; there remain a few cherished volumes. These include *The Fitness of the Environment* by L. J. Henderson, *From Fish to Philosopher* and *Kamongo* by H. W . Smith, and *McCance and Widdowson: A Scientific Partnership of 60 Years* (ed. by M. Ashwell). These are nostalgic reminders of my long-gone scientific life.

ESSAYS. The essay is a genre of writing that conveys personal experience or observation, combined with reflection on its meaning; at the same time it reveals something of the writer's personality. My favorite essayists are E. B. White, F. L. Lucas, Loren Eiseley, Lewis Thomas, Chet Raymo—all of whom delight and inform the modern scene. And for a multitude of nuggets there is Curtis and Greenslet's *The Practical Cogitator Or The Thinker's Anthology*—a veritable cerebral goldmine.

SCIENCE AND RELIGION. This brings us to that age-old issue confronting the human mind: the relation of the material world to the world of the spirit. We have, of course, *The Bible* (King James version preferred), the bulwark of my ancestors but admittedly less read by this scientist-descendant who long has been fascinated by some of the following books that attempt to reconcile science and religion. In my college years I was entranced by *The Mysterious Universe* by James Jeans and *The Nature of the Physical World* and *Science and the Unseen World* both by Arthur Eddington. A. N. Whitehead's *Science and the Modern World* emphasized the philosophical importance of "process". In later years there followed a host of metaphysical discussions by other scientists— paleontologists, biologists, physicists, astronomers, cosmologists: *The Phenomenon of Man* (Teilhard de Chardin), *You and the Universe* (N. J. Berrill), *Purpose in a World of Chance* (W. H. Thorpe), *The Way the World Is* (John Polkinghorne), *In the Centre of Immensities* (Bernard Lovell), *Infinite in All Directions* (Freeman Dyson), *A Brief History of Time* (Stephen Hawking), *The Emperor's New Mind* (Roger Penrose), *The Mind of God* (Paul Davies). The role of science in Christianity, and particularly in Quaker belief, is presented cogently by Kathleen Lonsdale in *The Christian Life—Lived Experimentally* and by Donald Court in *A Declining Church: What Has a Friend to Say?*

All the above books strive to relate the material world of the Big Bang, quantum mechanics, and the turbulent cosmos, to the world of the spirit, of purpose, meaning, and values; they all attest to the mystery of the Power that must lie behind it all.

REFERENCE. And finally, to come down to a more pragmatic note concerning the use of words, the building blocks of books. Dictionaries are essential for both the writer and the reader; I lean on *Webster's International Dictionary* (Second Edition) and the *Concise Oxford Dictionary*. For myself as a writer, two books are paramount: Fowler's *Modern English Usage* and Strunk and White's *The Elements of Style*. These books promote clarity of language in the words flowing from pen or word processor as books are written or indeed written about. Make it clear, make it readable!

*   *   *

So what is the role of books in the scheme of things? Books comprise symbols in the form of words that convey ideas from one human mind to other human minds. Thus books are the repositories and users of language, the hallmark of our species. Books are the surest, safest, most direct way for the reader to connect his or her mind—the world inside the head—with the world outside, with the "noosphere". The noosphere is the term applied by Teilhard de Chardin to the evergrowing mass of thoughts and ideas enveloping the globe—the "consciousness of the world" as Lewis Thomas calls it. Computer disks and electronic networks may increase the speed of communication within the noosphere but books are its permanent building blocks. As Clarence Day said in his praise of libraries:

> The world of books is the most remarkable creation
> of man;
> Nothing else that he builds ever lasts, monuments
> fall, nations perish, civilizations grow old and
> die out and, after an era of darkness, new rac-
> es build others;
> But in the world of books are volumes that have
> seen this happen again and again and yet live
> on, still young, still as fresh as the day they
> were written, still telling men's hearts of the
> hearts of men centuries dead.

July, 1993

THE LIFE OF THE IMAGINATION

Reading is a private activity and entails a private relationship between two people, reader and writer. It takes place over time unless the reader rejects the book. Spoken language can take short cuts, take cues from the respondent's face or situation. Written language is addressed to someone unknown—it makes an imagined world. . . out of one person's inner life and offers it to another separate person to experience and think about.

Reading is a means of encountering the world outside in a safe way in the world-in-the-head, which can give both experience and understanding. —A. B. Byatt, *Guardian Weekly*, March 15, 1992.

158

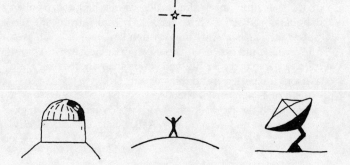

23

"Science and the Unseen World"

Quaker Scientists Look at Religion

One evening a dozen years ago, our two oldest grand-daughters, Miranda, then age 13 years, and Rebecca, age 10, quizzed their grandfather about the nature of the universe and what it all means. In response, I, as a medical scientist and Quaker, wrote and sent to them a paper entitled "One Quaker's Quest from Quarks to Quasars, the Universe and You and Me". Two years later, Rebecca apparently was not satisfied with my amateurish excursion into particle physics and cosmology and their possible religious implications. So,to ferret out further my religious beliefs, she sent me a questionnaire.

"To Grandaddy", she wrote, "This is a set of questions which I often wonder about. I would like to know what your thoughts and beliefs are. Please send them to me when you've answered them". There followed some seventeen questions ranging from "Who is God?" through such ones as "What is heaven?", "Can you believe in evolution and God?", Do you believe in the 'Christmas story'?", "If we are all *Homo sapiens*, built basically the same way, how can we hold prejudices against some and like others???", to "What are Quaker beliefs?". To these searching questions from the keen mind of a twelve-year-old, I sent the best answers I could muster, to supplement my comments in my "Quarks to Quasars" essay (published in my previous volume of essays, *Bird On A Rocking Chair*, 1988).

Questions such as these become rather more pressing to an octogenarian as, in his ninth decade, he undergoes the harsher vicissitudes that progressive old age brings to him and his beloved spouse in their approach to the end of life's road. So what *are* my beliefs?

Here am I, a person born and raised in a family that for many generations has belonged to the Religious Society of Friends (Quakers). My forbears in this family held strong Christian beliefs in the power of God and his love for all men. It was this belief, surely, that led to my great-grandfather's efforts to help native Indians, freed negro slaves, and refugee Russian Doukhobors, to my grandfather's travels in the ministry about the world including West China, (see earlier essays), to my father's life-long work during his business travels to unite groups of Quakers across the continent and—as one of the founders of the Friends World Committee for Consultation—around the world. How do I reconcile their strong Christian Quaker beliefs with my view of life and the world from my perspective as a physician and medical scientist?

But first, how have other scientists dealt with the dilemmas arising between their science and their religion? The 20th Century literature on this subject is hardly meager and ranges from reductionism and materialistic atheism, through agnosticism, to complete religious belief. Many scientists, as they search for a "grand unified theory" or a "theory of everything" in the physical world, consider religion to be a meta-physical subject lying outside their scientific expertise and so avoid discussion of the issue. But, as indicated in the list of books in the section on "Science and Religion" in the preceding essay in this volume, the dam of scientists' reticence has been broken. A series of eminent scientists—physicists, biologists, cosmologists—have striven to relate the material world of the Big Bang, quantum mechanics, and the turbulent cosmos to the world of spirit, of purpose, meaning, and values; they acknowledge the mystery of the Power that must lie behind it all. Two examples of this metaphysical trend may be given as follows.

Here is the conclusion of Stephen Hawking, mathematician and cosmologist, as expressed in his book *A Brief History of Time: From the Big Bang to Black Holes* (1988):

> Even if there is only one possible unified theory, it is just a set of rules and equations. What is it that breathes fire into the equations and makes a universe for them to describe? . . .Is the universe so compelling that it brings about its own existence? . . .Or does it need a creator? If we do discover a complete theory, . . .then we shall all be able to take part in the discussion of the question of why it is that we and the universe exist. If we can find the answer to that, . . .we would know the mind of God.

Paul Davies, physicist, in his book *The Mind of God* (1992), concludes:

> We, who are children of the universe—animated stardust—can nevertheless reflect on the nature of that same universe, even to the extent of glimpsing the rules on which it runs. . . .What does it mean? The physical species *Homo sapiens* may count for nothing, but the existence of mind. . .is surely a fact of fundamental significance. Through conscious beings the universe has generated self-awareness. This can be no trivial detail, no minor byproduct of mindless, purposeless forces. We are truly meant to be here.

What do Quaker scientists, members of the Religious Society of Friends, have to say, how do they relate their scientific perspective to their Quaker religious beliefs? Of a series of such scientists, primarily in Britain and America, I can quote from only a few.

Sir Arthur Eddington (1882-1944), FRS, astrophysicist and Professor of Astronomy at Cambridge University, in 1919 obtained, during a total solar eclipse in West Africa, the first direct evidence in support of Einstein's theory of general relativity, namely, that the gravity of a massive star (the sun) bent nearby paths of starlight. In 1929 he gave, to the London Yearly Meeting of the Society of Friends, the Swarthmore Lecture entitled "Science and the Unseen World" (which title I have borrowed, in quotation marks, for this essay). He pointed out that mind is the first and most direct thing in our experience, all else in remote inference. The "real" physical world is, at the bottom, symbols, and consciousness gives meaning to the symbolism. Thus, experience is not limited to sense impressions and scientific measurements. It also involves a reaching out to something beyond: truth, beauty, the poetry of existence—not measurable by the tools of science:

> It is of the very essence of the unseen world that the conception of personality should dominate it. . .We have to build the spiritual world out of symbols taken from our own personality as we build the physical world out of the symbols of the mathematician.

W. Russell (later, Lord) Brain (1895-1966), FRS, was an eminent Quaker physician and neurologist, student of the mind and perception, President of the Royal College of Physicians of London and of the British Association for the Advancement of Science. In his 1944 Swarthmore Lecture on "Man, Society, and Religion" he stated his belief that Quakers tend to underestimate the importance of thought in religious life, and that Quakerism offers a bridge between life of the mind and life of matter, between religion and modern scientific culture. In light comment on this theme of Russell Brain's, a member of the London Yearly Meeting wrote:

> If we give thought no proper part,
> Then semi-Quakers we remain,
> Besides a trembling of the heart
> We need a rustle of the brain.

The importance of mind and human thought again has been emphasized by William H. Thorpe, Quaker professor of biology and student of animal behavior. In his book *Purpose in a World of Chance: A Biologist's View* (1978) he is engaged with the emergence of purposiveness in life and in its highest level reached in the human mind and consciousness. The primacy of mind in nature, he says, cannot be a matter of mechanistic chance.

Kathleen Lonsdale (1903-1971), FRS, crystallographer and Professor of Chemistry at the University of London, was the first woman scientist to be elected to the Royal Society, to be President of the British Association, and to be made a Dame for her scientific achievements. In her Swarthmore Lecture of 1953 she emphasized the importance of experience in living experimentally as scientists in the material world and as seekers in the spiritual world. In defining the relation of science to Quakerism, she wrote (in 1956):

> Friends do not accept the idea that the universe occurred by chance, that man is a chance conglomeration of molecules which has developed ideals, a conscience, humanitarian instincts merely in order to survive. . . To attribute the creation of matter to a Supreme Spirit may be a way of expressing what we do not understand. . . But this is not enough. The Society of Friends is a Christian body of people who take Jesus Christ as their example and who think of God in terms of Christ's life

and teaching. . . This means the basing of the experiment of life on the assumption that God is a loving Heavenly Father who is accessible to man, who cares for man.

Joseph Stokes, Jr., (1896-1972) was Professor of Pediatrics at the University of Pennsylvania, Physician-in-Chief to the Children's Hospital of Philadelphia, a pioneer scientist in the field of the development of vaccines, and a great humanitarian. In a memorandum to a group of fellow Quaker doctors in 1968 he wrote:

> For three hundred years members of the Religious Society of Friends have been seekers of the "abundant life" for themselves and for their fellow men. Believing that the Supreme Power in the universe is good and that some portion of that Power lies as an "Inner Light" or "spark" within each human being, Quakers have ever attempted to cultivate this "spark" to the end that the quality of life of all men might be creative, satisfying, and mutually beneficial—a goal that is in accord with the Judeo-Christian ethic. . .
>
> Now, new powers to change the quality of life—powers conferred by the advances of biomedical science—pose questions to all men. . . Do not the answers to these dilemmas require the recognition that love—in the largest sense—and all the consequences that flow from it, is a necessary ingredient of the whole man and the abundant life?

These Quaker scientists, and many others, have been and are firm believers in the spiritual life and the experimental approach to truth. But they also have stressed the limitations of the methods of science in making the approach to the world of values. Some Quaker scientists and physicians have centered their religious life on the divinity of Christ, some on the message of love and forgiveness brought by a supremely wise but not necessarily divine Jesus, some on the mystical evolutionary force of whose process we and our universe are a part, and some, perhaps, have been frankly agnostic. But most Quaker scientists and physicians, know that along with beauty, goodness, and love in the world there is suffering, hate, and evil that derive from our evolutionary past. They appear to have based their lives on the central belief that, despite this inheritance from the past of suffering and evil, a caring God gives unity to all life, is potentially present in all human beings, and must be sought for continually to give strength to one's daily actions. This belief surely lies at the heart of the Quaker heritage in science and medicine.

With such writings by Quaker scientists and against the background of my own scientific life, I present a few of my answers to my granddaughter Rebecca's questions.

Who is God? I believe there is a power that exists both within and beyond our lives and the world and universe. It is a power that is continually creating us and the rest of reality, a power to which we human beings can turn for support and help even through we cannot understand it. Because this unseen spiritual power is a life force that touches our human personalities with love, humans in the past have talked of it in terms of parenthood, that is, as God the Father. But He/She is not a person and certainly is not of any one gender. However, because this mysterious power partakes of the quality of personality as we humans know it, I personally find it easier to think of, and try to communicate with, It/Him/Her in personal terms as "God" or "Lord."

Can you believe in evolution and God? Of course. There can be no doubt that life on earth has evolved over several billion years. And that is how He/She works as the creative life force, at least on this planet.

Do you believe in the "Christmas Story"? It is a beautiful story based on the joy of the birth of the historical Jesus. Its message is that "Yes, Rebecca, there is a Santa Claus", that is, the Babe was to bring the good news that there is hope and love in the world that can overcome evil.

What are the Quaker beliefs? As they have no fixed creed, Quakers hold many aspects of religious belief. The central theme was begun by George Fox who preached that there was part of the spirit of God in every man, that humans could speak and listen to God directly without a priest as a necessary intermediary, and that the loving spirit of God was most clearly revealed by the life of Jesus Christ. From those central beliefs stem the Quaker practices of meeting together in silent worship with ministry by any worshiper, of testimonies against all forms of violence including military service, and of relief and care for the needy and suffering peoples of the world.

If we are all Homo sapiens, built the same way, how can we hold prejudices against some and like others? We are not as "sapiens" as we might be or think we are. Evolving from lower forms of life, we have inherited in our subcortical brains (thalamus, limbic system) strong emotional instincts of tribe and territory that are hard to throw off. Humans just have to keep on trying to control and eventually to eliminate these instincts that lead to prejudices against others.

Do you think that God might flood the earth again if we get too evil? I am not sure that He/She really did the first time. But God has given humankind free will to choose and, if humans make the less good, wrong, or evil choices, they may bring on themselves enough evil consequences (such as nuclear holocaust or environmental degradation) to lead to extinction. But although it is getting harder to be one, I am still an optimist—I don't think that that is going to happen. I believe that the common sense and ingenuity of men will prevail, that the human race will continue to evolve, that love will triumph over hate, and that good will conquer evil. And to do that humans will need all the help that they can ask for from the mysterious power we call God.

"There, dear granddaughter, are my current answers to your questions, answers that surely are conditioned by the happy, loving family and fortunate life with which I have been blest. May similar blessings come to you. Affectionately, Gran'daddy. (Colwall, Herefordshire, January, 1984.)"

*   *   *

So here stands revealed the tenuous state of the religious beliefs of this aging scientist-descendant of a strong Christian Quaker line. His seems to be a not very "Christocentric" faith of "reasonable uncertainty", of mystical agnosticism. Despite having had no specific mystical experiences, he has a strong belief in "faith, hope, and love" as important ingredients in the great mystery of on-going creation. Perhaps the state of his spiritual life might be characterized (appropriately) in a reverse of the parodied terms of Russell Brain's diagnosis of the state of British Quakerdom: the author of this essay is suffering from too little "trembling of the heart" and too much "rustle of the brain".

Bedford, MA
May, 1994

P.S.: In 1931, while a student at Haverford College majoring in philosophy, I wrote a paper for my Quaker teachers, Rufus Jones and Douglas Steere, on the subject, "Does evolution support an interpretation of the universe as friendly to human values?". Without benefit of the theory of the Big Bang, particle physics, quantum mechanics, Heisenberg's uncertainty, or the anthropic principle, I made the case (at length) that it does. Apparently, more than 60 years of living since then have not made me change my mind.

"I never thought I'd make it.
Yet, here I am, a full fledged old man".

24

Bird in a Wheelchair

The Decelerating Years in a Home Away From Home

As an octogenarian who, with his wife, has spent nearly four of his "decelerating" years in a very well-organized and well-run continuing care retirement community (CCRC), I offer these reflections about our "home away from home".

Modern retirement homes that provide continuing or life care are springing up all over the country. Care in these institutions ranges from living in independent units to full-time medical or nursing care at all levels. Because of their cost CCRCs of necessity only serve the more affluent aging members of the middle class. Setting aside, for the moment, the wider problem of health care for the much greater number of the nation's less-affluent elderly, what are the advantages and disadvantages of these protective "cocoons" for those of us who are able to afford them?

The advantages of the CCRC are clear and are the

reasons why we spend our money to enter them. They provide food, shelter, and the assurance of care at a time when, in
this physically and mentally decelerating phase of our lives,
we need it. In this day and age both our children and their
spouses usually have full-time professional careers in addition to raising their own children. They have their own lives
to live and we wish to spare them the burden of having to
care for us as well. Of course we want to see as much of them
as possible—that is why we generally try to choose a CCRC in
their vicinity.

Social contacts are important as they mitigate the loneliness that threatens the elderly when many old friends and
acquaintances no longer are at hand. In the more than 300 residents in our community there is a tremendous variety of personalities and life-time experiences, all waiting to be shared.
As would be expected, women greatly outnumber men, as do
widows over widowers and married couples. The more gre-
garious find ample opportunity for socializing, the less gre-
garious can go at their own pace according to temperament.
Stimulating new friends and acquaintances indeed are at
hand.

To catalyze, educate, and entertain this social mixture
there are a multitude of activities. These include lectures, concerts, movies, parties, receptions, bridge tournaments, Garden
Club meetings, as well as off-campus trips to Symphony, mu-
seums, historic and scenic sites. Sports are available (croquet,
miniature golf, billiards, pool) as well as exercise sessions,
craft classes, and a woodworking shop. For the more independent and able there are walking on the many paths
around our pleasant country campus, the tending of small
personal flower gardens, and bird watching. For the less mobile in armchair, wheelchair, or bed, there is reading; the excellent library is one of the focal points in our community. For
those in need of religious support (and who is not?) church

services are conducted weekly by our full-time chaplain or by invited outside ministers.

A strong Residents Association maintains, through its executive officers and Council, a continuing close link with the Executive Director and her staff. Committees of the Association provide ample opportunity for residents to participate in promoting the smooth running of our community.

Good medical care is a *sine qua non* of any CCRC. Here it is well provided by the full-time Medical Director and nursing staff, supplemented by visiting consultants and liaisons with hospitals in the surrounding area. Nutritional supervision and counselling are given by a registered dietitian. Our Health Center contains 120 beds at four levels of nursing care and serves patients from the local community as well as the residents of the CCRC. For the "decelerating" residents, quality of all the staff is of the highest importance. In this we are extremely fortunate in our Executive Director and senior administrators, in our staff at all levels, as well as in our independent Board of Trustees. They care! What a rosy picture of our "home away from home"!

Are there then, in this Garden of Eden for the elderly, if no snakes, at least mosquitoes? Are there flies in the ointment? Of course there are.

Modern CCRCs by their very nature segregate their elderly inhabitants and thus, to a certain extent, isolate them from younger generations. One critic has termed such establishments "protected ghettos for the affluent elderly". This is much too severe. We are not surrounded by an impregnable wall but by a very efficient semi-permeable membrane. Daily younger people on the staff flow in and out, cheering us immensely as they look after our needs. Equally importantly, our families—children, grandchildren, and even a few "great-grands"—bring love and cheer and maintenance of family ties. In addition, frequent sorties off campus help to keep us in touch with the world. No, isolation is not much of a "fly in the ointment".

The predominant "beastie" in the Garden is that common condition of all humanity: the inexorable winding down of life into death. The rate of this winding down may vary greatly between body and mind, between husband and wife, between person and person, but sooner or later there comes full-stop. It is a scenario that here is played out over and over to the audience of fellow residents. We see friends having to make the much-feared transition from independent units to assisted living quarters, to nursing beds in the Health Center, to hospital; we see them reduced to walkers and wheelchairs; we see spouses or friends become depressed or sink into the never-never land of Alzheimer's disease. Finally, the cycle of life with all its vicissitudes will be completed in the release of death. What follows we do not know—that is a matter, not of knowledge, but of belief.

What a gloomy picture all this paints of our Garden of Eden. But this is only part of the picture. Our community is a very caring place, the staff cares for the residents and the residents care for each other. Everyday we see all around us enduring courage, bravery, and grace, as difficulties and illnesses are encountered. Everyday we learn again the truth of the aphorism "Old age is not for sissies". Everyday during our own crises we are supported by our fellow deceleratees. Nevertheless, all is not heartache and sorrow, there are fun and games here too as together we face the "beastie" in the Garden.

Perhaps a little humor is not amiss as we share our hopes and fears in this phase of our lives. To this end I present herewith, as a pictorial commentary, a few cartoons and drawings that were put together—perhaps rather blithely—at an earlier time before my wife and I were quite so close to the figurative "bird in a wheelchair". Herein are depicted some of the collisions between the dream, the myth, of the fountain of youth and the inexorable reality of the one-way flow of the sands of time. Perforce, we must laugh at ourselves lest we drown in our tears. Or at least smile. Here they are.

Late middle age:
complacency, or how
to bury your head in
the sand while lying
on your back

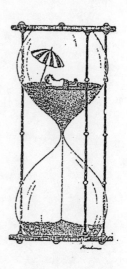

The rat race - time to retire?

"Taxes are up, population is up,
pollution is up, crime is up,
and now it's my blood pressure."

Yes, time to retire and to pass
the torch—and the problems
—on to those who follow

"That's it. I've taught you
everything I know."

Retirement —initial stage:
the fountain of youth,
euphoria, FREE!

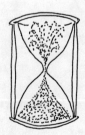

But reality soon sets in,
  followed by wisdom—perhaps

"There is no fountain of youth. This is
  the fountain of aging gracefully."

Acceptance *is the secret*

Then, the physical underprops
  begin to go.

"You've got termites in your prop!"

Time to see the doctor again —
    time is running out

Finally —
    full-stop
      release,
        takeoff

For drawings and ideas the author is grateful to the following cartoonists: Krahn, Censor, Hurit, P. Steiner, Peros, and Marino.

* * *

Lest the foregoing depictions of our decelerating and final years appear shallow, fatalistic, or unfeeling, I hasten to go beyond *acceptance* tinged with humor as the sole secret of aging gracefully. Whatever may be one's religious and philosophical beliefs, whether one is a believer in a personal God, an agnostic and mystic sensible of the mysterious Power behind and within the ongoing creation, or a humanist whose belief rests in the human spirit, the power of love is paramount. And its strength is to be found especially in the love and prayers of family and friends.

So, dwell not on the future, yearn not for the past, but accept the present, seize the moment, live a day at a time, work on a project, do things with others, savor the "dear gift of life". Then perhaps a few lingering drops of the fountain of youth will moisten the last departing grains of the sands of time. Then perhaps you will find the "fountain of age".

Carleton-Willard Village
Bedford, MA
August, 1993

Epilogue

The production of this second volume of essays involving the collection of ones written earlier and the writing of others more recently, has indeed moistened with a few lingering drops of the fountain of youth my own departing grains of the sands of time. To evoke scenes and ideas from an abundant past life is to bolster acceptance of the ever-increasing restrictions that have come to my wife and myself in these late "decelerating years".

Sooner or later on this planet death comes to all forms of life—this is nature's natural rhythm. Only in this way can ongoing successive generations evolve new forms of life. We are part of this process. What happens to individual minds and personalities after death, we do not know. I can only quote again from George Eliot's poem on immortality (as I did in the epilogue to my first volume of essays):

> Oh, may I join the choir invisible
> Of those immortal dead who live again
> In minds made better by their presence
> . . .This is the life to come. . .

We do live on—however briefly—in the minds and memories of those who come after us. By then we will have played our part in the "uninterrupted poem of creation, the morning wind that forever blows" and can rest in peace.

READINGS IN REFERENCE

3   *"Genetics and Ironing": the Two Cultures and the Physician*

C.P. Snow: *The Two Cultures and the Scientific Revolution.* Cambridge Univ. Press, New York, 1959.

9   *A Clear Day in Shropshire*

Mary Webb: *Precious Bane.* Jonathan Cape, London, 1928, 320 pages.
——*The Golden Arrow.* Jonathan Cape, London, 1928, 352 pages.

10   *Editor Garland and* The New England Journal of Medicine

Joseph Garland, M.D.: *A Time for Remembering.* Massachusetts Medical Society, Boston, 1972, 203 pages.

12   *The Case of the Itching Tattoo*

Arthur Conan Doyle: "The Red-headed League" and *"The Glo-*

ria Scott", in *The Complete Sherlock Holmes*. Garden City
Publishing Co., Garden City, New York, 1927, pages 194
and 429.

15   *Watching a Pair of Lesser White-Crested Birdwatchers*

E.B. White: "Mr. Forbush's Friends", in *Essays of E.B. White*,
Harper & Row, New York, 1977, pages 262-277.
Roger Tory Peterson, James Fisher: *Wild America*. Houghton
Mifflin Co., Boston, 1955, 434 pages.

17   *From Crete to Arizona, Gathering Time*

Mary Renault: *The King Must Die*. Pantheon Books, Inc., New
York, 1958, 338 pages.
Erma J. Fisk: *The Peacocks of Baboquivari*. W.W. Norton & Co.,
New York, London, 1983, 284 pages.
Willa Cather: *Death Comes for the Archbishop*. Alfred A. Knopf,
New York, 1927, 299 pages.
John McPhee: *Basin and Range*. Farrar-Straus-Giroux, New
York, 1980, 216 pages.
Stephen W. Hawking: *A Brief History of Time: From the Big
Bang to Black Holes*. Bantam Books, New York, 1988, 198
pages.
Stephen Jay Gould: *Time's Arrow, Time's Cycle: Myth and Meta-
phor in the Discovery of Geological Time*. Harvard Uni-
versity Press, Cambridge, MA, 1987, 222 pages.

18   *Doctors Far Afield*

John McPhee: Ibid (Essay 17).
Stephen Jay Gould: Ibid (Essay 17).
E.F. Norton: *Fight for Everest.* Longman, Green & Co., New
   York, 1925.
John Noel: *The Story of Everest.* Little, Brown, & Co., New
   York, 1927.

19   *The Rise and Decline of the Age of Antibiotics*

Science, vol. 257, 21 August, 1992: Articles on antibiotic re-
   sistance and microbial wars, by D.E. Koshland, Jr., and
   others, pages 1021, 1036-39, 1050-82.
Richard Preston: A Reporter at Large: Crisis in the Hot Zone.
   The New Yorker, October 26, 1992, pages 58-81.
Stephen S. Morse, Robert D. Brown: The Enemy Within: As
   civilization spreads, so do viruses. *Modern Maturity,*
   June-July, 1993, pages 50-54.
Science, vol. 264, 15 April, 1994: Articles on antibiotic re-
   sistance and the biological warfare of the future, by D.E.
   Koshland, Jr., and others, pages 327, 360-393.

20   *From Brown Eggs to the Loch Ness Monster*

Anthony Trollope: *The Warden,* 1855, Ch. 8.
A.A. Milne: *Winnie-The-Pooh.* E.P. Dutton & Co., New York,
   1926, 159 pages.
Constance Whyte: *More Than a Legend.* London, Hamish
   Hamilton, 1957, 1961.

Tim Dinsdale: *Loch Ness Monster*. London, Routledge and Kegan Paul, 1976 (3rd edition), 171 pages.

Henry H. Bauer: *The Enigma of Loch Ness: Making Sense of a Mystery*. Urbana and Chicago, University of Illinois Press, 1986, 243 pages.

21   Quakers and the Russian Bear

R. Hingston Fox: *Dr. John Fothergill and His Friends: Chapters on Eighteenth Century Life*. Macmillan & Co., London, 1919, Ch. 9: Baron Dimsdale - Inoculation for Smallpox.

John Ormerod Greenwood: *Quaker Encounters*, William Sessions, York, 1977, Vol. 2, Ch. 7: Daniel Wheeler and the Quaker Pioneers in Russia.

———: Ibid, Vol. 1, Ch. 8: Friends and Russia in the late nineteenth century; the great famines and the Mennonite and Dukhobor migrations.

Griselda Fox Mason: *Sleigh Ride to Russia*. William Sessions, York, 1985, 120 pages.

Richenda C. Scott: *Quakers in Russia*, Michael Joseph, London, 1964.

John Bellows: Letters and Memoir, ed. by Elizabeth Bellows, Henry Holt & Co., New York, 1904, 392 pages.

Selections from the Diary and Correspondence of Joseph S. Elkinton, 1830-1905. Philadelphia, privately printed, Leeds & Biddle Co., 1913, 512 pages.

Joseph Elkinton: *The Doukhobors: Their History in Russia, Their Migration to Canada*. Ferris & Leach, Philadelphia, 1903, 336 pages.

23 *"Science and the Unseen World"*: Quaker Scientists Look at Religion

Stephen W. Hawking: Ibid (Essay 17).

Paul Davies: *The Mind of God: The Scientific Basis for a Rational World*. Simon & Schuster, New York, London, 1992, 254 pages.

Arthur S. Eddington: *Science and the Unseen World*. Macmillan Co., New York, 1929, 91 pages.

Kathleen Lonsdale: *Science and Quakerism*. Friends Home Service Committee, London, 1956, 7 pages.

———: *The Christian Life — Lived Experimentally*. Ibid, 1976, 59 pages.

David Murray-Rust: *God in the Universe: a twentieth century Quaker looks at science and theology*. Friends Home Service Committee, London, 1973, 60 pages.

William H. Thorpe: *Purpose in a World of Chance: A Biologist's View*. Oxford University Press, Oxford, London, New York, 1979, 124 pages.

J. Russell Elkinton: One Quaker's Quest from Quarks to Quasars: The Universe and You and Me, Essay 31 in *Bird on a Rocking Chair*. Cottage Press, Lincoln, MA, 1988, pages. 216-233.

——— with Robert A. Clark: *The Quaker Heritage in Medicine*: Boxwood Press, Pacific Grove, CA, 1978, 87 pages.

24 *Bird In a Wheel Chair: The Decelerating Years in a Home Away From Home*

Ruth M. Fawell: The Later Years—I, *The Friend* (London), Aug. 25, 1967, 1061-62; Loneliness—II, ibid, Sept. 1, 1967, 1087-88; The Last Loss—III, ibid, Sept. 8, 1967, 1121-22.

Mary C. Morrison: *Without Nightfall Upon the Spirit: Reflections On Aging.* Pamphlet 311, Pendle   Hill Publications, Wallingford, PA, 1993, 30 pages.

M. Andrew Greganti, MD: Life Care At Golden Acres, *Annals of Internal Medicine,* vol. 117, 15 Nov., 1992, 867-868.

Betty Friedan: *The Fountain of Age.* Simon & Schuster, New York, 1993, 671 pages.

Epilogue

Bradford Smith: *Dear Gift of Life: A Man's Encounter With Death.* Pamphlet 142, Pendle Hill Publications, Wallingford, PA, 1965, 38 pages.

About the Author

Dr. J. Russell Elkinton, a graduate of Haverford College and Harvard Medical School (1937), has spent most of his academic medical life in Philadelphia. After his internship and residency at the Pennsylvania Hospital and his postgraduate training in the field of metabolic and renal diseases at Yale School of Medicine, he became a staff physician, teacher, and clinical investigator in the Medical School and Hospital of the University of Pennsylvania. From 1960 to 1971 he served also as Editor of the *Annals of Internal Medicine* for the American College of Physicians.

In 1972 Dr. Elkinton and his wife, Teresa, retired to live in her native England. In 1985 they returned to Massachusetts to be near their children and grandchildren and now reside in a retirement community in Bedford. They both are members of the Religious Society of Friends.